THE OXFORD FUNNY STORY BOOK

Dennis Pepper

Oxford University Press

CONTENTS

Oxford University Press
Walton Street, Oxford OX2 6DP
Oxford • New York
Athens • Auckland • Bangkok • Bombay • Calcutta • Cape Town
Dar es Salaam • Delhi • Florence • Hong Kong • Istanbul • Karachi • Kuala Lumpur • Madras
Madrid • Melbourne • Mexico City • Nairobi • Paris • Singapore • Taipei • Tokyo • Toronto
and associated companies in
Berlin • Ibadan

Oxford is a trade mark of Oxford University Press

A CIP catalogue record for this book is available from the British Library

ISBN 0 19 278142 1 (hardback)
ISBN 0 19 278143 X (paperback)

Printed in Italy by G. Canale & C. S.p.A. - Borgaro T.se - TURIN

Thank you, St Joseph's

DENNIS HAMLEY

One hundred and thirty-four children looked at the man: the man looked at the one hundred and thirty-four children.

'This is a *celebrity*,' said Mrs Plunger. 'What is he, children?'

'A ce-*leb*-rity,' intoned one hundred and thirty-three voices.

'That's right,' said Mrs Plunger. 'And what did we say a ce-*leb*-rity is?'

Silence.

'Come on, we had this word in assembly yesterday.'

Deepening silence.

'Jake?'

Jake, at the back in the middle of Year 6, woke up suddenly.

'Like a footballer,' he said. 'Or a pop star. Or a fashion model.'

The other hundred and thirty-three faces peered doubtfully at the small, balding man standing in front of them. Which one was he?

'That's right, Jake,' said Mrs Plunger. 'But there are other sorts. Mr Finchingford is a *writer*.'

Jake looked unimpressed. Half a second later, the other hundred and thirty-three children were unimpressed as well.

'Mr Finchingford's here *all* day and he's going to talk to *everybody*. Say good morning to Mr Finchingford.'

'*Good-mor-ning-Mr-Fin-ching-ford.*'

One hundred and thirty-four voices.

'*Good-mor-ning-ev-ery-bo . . .*'

The infants' addition died out through lack of support.

'Mr Finchingford wants to say a few words now,' said Mrs Plunger.

He stepped forward.

'Well, yes,' he said. 'I do rather. I've got to write this story, you see. It's supposed to be funny. You've no idea how hard it is trying to be funny for kids. I can't think of anything funny *at all*. So I just wondered if you could tell me some things you thought were funny. Because if you think they're funny, so might other children. Do you see?'

Yes, they saw all right—so well that hands shooting in the air made a swooshing noise and the hall resounded with cries of *'Miss!'*

'I'm not a miss,' said Mr Finchingford.

Mrs Plunger quelled the uprising.

'You've been asked a sensible question and I want you to *think* about it. Mr Finchingford will see you all today, ending with Year 6. So put your hands down and keep your ideas to yourselves till then.'

They filed out.

'I'll tell him nothing,' said Jake. 'He should do his own work.'

Late afternoon came. Mr Finchingford was tired. Nobody had told him anything he could use. But Year 6 were the oldest, weren't they? So they should have some ideas.

Here they were, staring curiously as he was ushered in front of them. Sitting in the middle, stern-faced, arms folded, was a boy, bigger than the others, with black hair and dangerous eyes.

'That's Jake,' whispered Miss Cork. 'Get him on your side and everything's all right.'

Mr Finchingford talked and read for half an hour. Jake was definitely not on his side.

But the rest were. Especially when he said, 'Have you any ideas for me?'

'Not all at once,' said Miss Cork. 'Victoria?'

Victoria stood up.

'I've got an idea about this man called Bob and his hair changes wherever he goes. So when he's in school his hair changes to slugs and when he's on the farm it's worms and when he goes to the swimming pool it's frogs.'

Nobody laughed except Victoria herself and Karen next to her who was nearly hysterical.

'Then what happens?' said Mr Finchingford.

'Bob does lots of things,' said Victoria.

'What sort of things?'

'Different things.'

'Rubbish,' said Jake.

Karen stopped laughing and kicked him.

'Imogen? Claire?' said Miss Cork. 'They always do things together,' she whispered to Mr Finchingford.

Claire said, 'You could have a ghost who's all hippy and he wears ear-rings and a necklace and he's got green and blue hair and I've done a drawing of him and here it is . . .'

She waved a sheet of paper around.

'. . . And he could live in a little village in Japan,' said Imogen. 'And they've invented this game called Virtual Sumo Wrestling and there's this *really* weedy little boy who wants to play . . .'

'. . . So he goes to the hippy ghost for help and the ghost says . . .'

'Pathetic,' said Jake.

But Imogen and Claire were clinging to each other, too weak to continue.

'David?' said Miss Cork.

'Yeah,' said David. 'This is about Superblob and Evilblob and Evilblob's got this kryptonite photodisintegrator and he's going to destroy Earth with it but Superblob finds out and does a bellyflop right on Evilblob's rocket and . . .'

'This is *funny*?' said Jake.

''Course it is,' said David. 'It's dead funny.'

Jake inclined his eyes significantly towards the ceiling.

'Melanie,' said Miss Cork quickly.

'Mine's about a teacher with a punk haircut and he teaches the children how to cut their hair like that and when they go to Tesco's one boy throws a custard pie at his friend and then there's a food fight and there's food flung everywhere and . . .'

Everyone laughed except Jake, who said, 'I don't believe this' very loudly.

'I think this had better be the last one,' said Miss Cork desperately. 'Donna?'

'This is the story of Farmer Grumps,' said Donna. 'One morning he got out of bed the wrong side and everything went wrong. When he

went to feed the pigs he fell head first in the pigsty (poor Farmer Grumps). And then he had a special visitor. It was the mayor. When Farmer Grumps got up his trousers fell down and you could see his pants. They were white with red dots. Then Farmer Grumps heard a car pulling up. It was the mayor. Farmer Grumps was so embarrassed he went red and the mayor was gobsmacked.'

By now, Donna was weak with mirth and so were the four girls round her. Jake fixed them with a look of sheer contempt.

'What a load of garbage,' he said.

'I'm afraid it's time,' said Miss Cork.

Mr Finchingford cast a final, baffled look at Year 6.

'Thank you, St Joseph's,' he said and shuffled out.

Outside the school, everyone turned on Jake.

'That was *rotten*,' shrieked Donna.

Imogen and Claire started thumping him on the back.

'Get *off*,' he roared.

'You need a good duffing up,' yelled David.

'Come on, then,' said Jake. David hardly reached his shoulders.

Melanie stood in front of him, staring him out.

'At least we tried,' she said. 'You only pick holes.'

'I could do better than you,' said Jake. 'If I'd wanted.'

'Go on, then,' said Victoria.

'What's the point? He won't use anything you said.'

'How do you know?' said Claire.

'Because he won't,' said Jake.

'He might,' said Imogen.

'Whose?' said Jake.

'Mine,' said Victoria.

'Ours,' said Imogen and Claire.

'There you are,' said Jake. 'How can he choose?'

'Because mine's the best,' said David.

Suddenly David, not Jake, was the object of the girls' violence.

'He only wanted one story,' said Jake. 'If you'd put all those bits together . . .'

'That's silly,' said Victoria.

'No, it's not,' said Jake. 'Let's try it and see.'

'All right,' said Imogen. 'What if Farmer Grumps got out of bed the wrong side and his hair had turned into *worms . . .*'

'But it's Bob who's got funny hair,' said Victoria.

'We'll have to get rid of some bits if we're going to make one story,' said Jake.

'Well, you're not getting rid of my Bob,' said Victoria stubbornly.

'We can keep his hair,' said Imogen.

'Farmer Grumps could go for help to the teacher who's teaching children punk haircutting,' said Melanie.

'Why?' demanded David. 'Why doesn't he go straight to Superblob? He's the only one who can sort this mess out.'

'That's stupid,' said Claire. 'Superblob's got *nothing* to do with this story.'

'Nor have daft hippy ghosts,' said David.

'But what about Farmer Grumps?' wailed Donna. 'Why should his hair be all sluggy and wormy? What about when the mayor comes?'

'If the mayor doesn't like it, Farmer Grumps can challenge him to a Sumo wrestling match,' said Imogen.

'Or throw Tesco custard pies at him,' said Melanie.

'It's not fair,' said Victoria. 'I want my Bob and his sluggy hair back.'

'And I want my Farmer Grumps with his ordinary hair,' said Donna.

'SHUT UP!' roared Jake. 'You're not trying, any of you.'

They quietened down.

'Think about it,' said Jake. 'We'll meet in the playground before school tomorrow. I'm sure we can do it.'

So they did.

Next morning, Miss Cork found a roomful of attentive, expectant sixth years. Jake stood up.

'They've got a story to tell you,' he said.

The others stood up as well. Jake faced them like an orchestra conductor.

'Victoria first,' he said.

'This is the story of Farmer Grumps,' said Victoria. 'One morning he got out of bed the wrong side and his hair had turned into worms in the night . . .'

'Imogen.'

'. . . And he was so scared he ran outside and fell in the pigsty and he shouted "I've got to get rid of my wormy hair because the mayor's coming" . . .'

'Now Melanie.'

'. . . So he went to a teacher with a punk haircut who'd just finished teaching the children how to do it. By now his hair had turned to slugs so they tried to cut it like a punk's but it just ended up a mass of slugs on top of his head . . .'

'David.'

'. . . So the teacher said, "We've got to do better than this. Send for *Superblob*" and Superblob came and said, "There's only one thing can get rid of the slugs and that's Evilblob's kryptonite photodisintegrator" . . .'

'Donna.'

'. . . "But *you'll* have to get it off him because kryptonite is fatal to me," said Superblob. "What can we do against Evilblob?" wailed Farmer Grumps and the teacher. "We're so little and weak." And Superblob said, "There's just one chance. I know this Japanese village where they've invented Virtual Sumo Wrestling and the littlest, weediest one of the lot is champion. I'll get him for you" . . .'

'Your turn, Claire.'

'. . . So off he went at the speed of light and ten minutes later he came back with this little weedy boy and a computer and lots of virtual reality helmets and Superblob said, "Put these on and wait for Evilblob because I'll lure him here" . . .'

'Victoria again.'

'. . . And they put the helmets on and it was all weird because they saw the punk ghost who lived in the village with his waistcoats and ear-rings and necklaces and he said, "I'll help you beat Evilblob" and Superblob shouted, "Look out! Evilblob's coming" . . .'

'Imogen.'

'. . . And Evilblob had the photodisintegrator and he said, "I won't just disintegrate your sluggy hair, I'll disintegrate you *all*" . . .'

'It's you Melanie.'

'. . . And the hippy ghost said. *"Now!"* and Farmer Grumps and the teacher and all the children swelled up so they were the biggest Sumo Wrestlers you ever saw . . .'

'David.'

'. . . And Evilblob laughed and he said, "You can't frighten me. I can blob the lot of you just like that." And Superblob flew overhead and he said, "Oh, no, it's not going to work. I'll have to do a bellyflop" . . .'

'Donna.'

'. . . And so he did, but he missed and squashed them all into Tesco's custard pies . . .'

'Claire.'

'And just then the mayor came up and all he found left was a bit of Farmer Grumps's pants . . .'

'All together now,' said Jake.

'AND THEY WERE WHITE WITH RED DOTS!'

'Lovely,' said Miss Cork. 'Write it down and send it to Mr Finchingford.'

'Ne-*ver*!' shouted the six storytellers.

'Let him think up his own stories,' said Jake.

And they all sat down, feeling very pleased.

The Hodja and the Poisoned Baklava

TRADITIONAL

Once, when the Hodja was standing in for the village schoolmaster, he was sent a large box of baklava by the parents of one of his students. His mouth watered at the thought of eating them, but he put them away in the drawer of his desk. Shortly afterwards he was called out on urgent business.

He set his students a lot of work to do.

'And I shall expect you to get everything right,' he said, 'or there will be trouble.' He glared at them. 'Big trouble.'

'One thing more,' he said as he made for the door. 'I have enemies. Many enemies. I keep being sent poisoned meats and poisoned sweets. Even,' he added fiercely, 'poisoned baklava. I have to test everything before I eat it. So be warned. If you hope for a long life, don't touch anything that has been sent to me. Especially baklava.'

As soon as he had gone, his nephew, who was one of his students, went to the desk and took out the baklava.

'Don't!' his friends shouted. 'They may be poisoned!'

The boy grinned at them.

'Of course they aren't,' he said. 'He just wants to keep them for himself.' And he started in on the baklava. 'They really are very good,' he said. He ate another one.

When his friends saw that he didn't fall to the floor in a writhing heap they gathered round the Hodja's desk and shared out the baklava.

'But what will we tell him when he finds they've all gone?' one of them said, wiping the crumbs from his mouth.

The Hodja's nephew just smiled.

When the Hodja returned, he went straight to his desk and looked in his drawer. He glared at his students.

'Someone,' he said, 'someone has been at my desk.'

There was silence.

'Someone has been in my drawer.'

Silence.

'And someone has eaten the baklava.'

'I have,' said his nephew.

'*You* have! After what I told you?'

'Yes.'

'Perhaps you have some explanation. If so, I would like to hear it before you die.'

'Well,' said his nephew, 'the work you set was far too hard for me. I couldn't do any of it. Everything I've done is wrong. I knew you would be very angry and my parents would be very disappointed. I felt so ashamed I decided that the only thing to do was to . . . to . . . to put an end to my life. So I ate your poisoned baklava. It was the only way I could think of on the spur of the moment. But the funny thing is, nothing's happened yet. I wonder why that is.'

The Hodja examined his nephew's innocent expression minutely.

'Perhaps,' he said, 'it's just a punishment postponed. In which case I ought to have a look at what work you have done.'

Excuses, Excuses

Andrew Matthews

Not long after the roof blew off Wyvern Copse School, Two Red noticed that there was a battle going on. The battle was between Gerry Atkins and Mr Haggerty, Two Red's French teacher, and it was about homework: or rather, the lack of it.

It was a surprising struggle. Gerry was a pear-shaped boy with brown hair and freckles whose only outstanding quality was his unremarkability; Mr Haggerty was a large man with a mane of white hair, bristling eyebrows and a reputation for prickliness. He was particularly prickly when it came to homework and was Master of the Awkward Question.

'I couldn't do the exercise you set us last night, I didn't understand it, sir,' would be met with, 'Then where is the work you did instead?'

Any pupil honest enough to admit forgetting homework would be given verbs to write out. Mr Haggerty took pains to point out that the verbs were not a punishment but an aid to the memory.

The first time Gerry Atkins failed to do his French, he had a genuine enough excuse—he had been ill when it was set. Mr Haggerty had nodded sympathetically and said that Gerry would have to do a double homework to make up for the time he had lost.

Gerry was aggrieved by this.

'It's not fair!' he complained loudly to his mate, Tim Worcester. 'He's punishing me because I was ill! It wasn't my fault!'

14

'It was in a way,' said Tim. 'You told me it was all those Mexican beans you ate.'

'I was hungry!' Gerry countered. 'I like Mexican beans! I didn't know that eating two lots would turn me into a human aerosol can the next day, did I? Now I've got double French homework because of it! That Haggerty bloke isn't human!'

'Of course he isn't,' Tim agreed. 'He's a teacher.'

Gerry set his jaw and squinted determinedly. 'Well, I'm not doing it! He can whistle for his precious homework!'

'But, Gerry!' squeaked Tim. 'It's Mr Haggerty!'

'I know.'

'Winding him up is like juggling with nitro-glycerine! Just do the extra work! A quiet life's better than a noisy, painful death!'

'No!' said Gerry. 'This is a matter of principle!'

Battle was joined in the next French lesson. When Mr Haggerty asked for the books to be handed in, Gerry's hand went up in the air like the tail of a cat who has just heard a tin being opened.

'Ah, Atkins!' smiled Mr Haggerty. 'You're about to give in two home-works, aren't you?'

'No, sir,' said Gerry. 'I haven't done any homework at all, sir.'

Mr Haggerty's smile stayed fixed but his eyes narrowed. 'Why not, Atkins?'

'We had a power cut last night, sir.'

Power cuts had been frequent since the Great October Storm and it was not the first time that Mr Haggerty had dealt with this particular excuse.

'Didn't you have any candles in your house, Atkins?'

'Yes, sir, a boxful, sir!' responded Gerry.

'Then why didn't you do your homework by candlelight?' concluded Mr Haggerty triumphantly.

'Well, sir,' began Gerry, 'the thing is, the box of candles was in the garden shed. My mum sent me out to get them. I was bringing them back into the house when I tripped over and they went flying. It was so dark because of the power cut, I couldn't find them, sir!'

If Mr Haggerty had been a dog, he would have growled; as it was he frowned severely and when he spoke, the temperature of his voice was well below zero.

'I'm going to give you the benefit of the doubt, Atkins, and believe you. This time. You will do both homeworks by Friday and show them to me at the start of the lesson.'

'My granny's coming to stay, sir!' said Gerry hurriedly.

Mr Haggerty looked puzzled. 'A fascinating snippet of information, Atkins, whose relevance, for the moment, eludes me!'

'Well, you see, sir, my granny's a bit funny—'

'I don't care if she's an award-winning comedienne, laddie!' roared Mr Haggerty. 'Get those homeworks done, or else!'

In registration on Friday morning, Gerry and Tim were approached by Wayne Armitage, Two Red's wheeler-dealer.

'You done that French then, Atko?' he asked confidentially.

'No.'

Wayne whistled.

'You gotta lotta bottle, kid,' he said. 'Either that or you're a complete wally! Anyway, fancy a little flutter?'

'Flutter?' echoed Gerry.

'You know, a bet!' Wayne explained.

'A bet on what?'

'5p stake,' said Wayne. 'Two-to-one, you gets put in detention. Five-to-one, 'Aggerty drags you straight down to the 'Ead!'

'What if he lets me off?' asked Gerry.

Wayne laughed, ''Aggerty let you off? Ten-to-one chance, mate!'

'Right!' said Gerry, digging in his pocket for a five pence piece. 'You're on!'

The atmosphere was tense at the start of French. All eyes were fixed on Gerry as, with a flourish, he set his exercise book down on Mr Haggerty's table. Mr Haggerty leafed through the book and his eyes bulged.

'What's the meaning of this, Atkins?' he rasped. 'Your homework is still not done!'

'I tried to tell you the last time, sir! My granny's staying with us.'

'Atkins,' seethed Mr Haggerty, 'I'm going to ask you a simple question, but I want you to think carefully about your answer, because it could be your last words! What does your grandmother have to do with it?'

'She hates anything to do with France, sir! She suffers from Francophobia.'

'What?' shrieked Mr Haggerty.

'Anything to do with France gives her one of her turns, sir,' said Gerry. 'She trampled the remote control on our telly last year when Delia Smith did a recipe for coq au vin. I can't do any French homework while she's in the house, sir.'

Mr Haggerty tried to speak several times, without success. When his voice eventually emerged, it was strangled, as though he were doing to his vocal cords what he would like to do to Gerry.

'Atkins, when is your grandmother leaving?'

'Tonight, sir.'

'Very well. Over the weekend, you'll do the two homeworks you owe me, plus the one I'm setting this lesson. You'll show them to me on Monday. And . . . Atkins?'

'Sir?'

'If you're taken ill, dictate your homework to a nurse!' snapped Mr Haggerty. 'If the illness proves fatal, dictate it to a medium!'

At the end of the lesson, Wayne Armitage paid Gerry fifty pence. He was grinning broadly as he did it.

'Magic!' he exclaimed admiringly.

'What are you so happy about?' Gerry demanded. 'Does losing money appeal to your sense of humour, or something?'

'Who's losin' money?' beamed Wayne. 'Twenty kids in our class bet that you'd get put in detention! I'm 50p up on the deal! I'm openin' another book for Monday. Two-to-one you do the 'omework, ten-to-one you don't do it and you gets a detention!'

'What if I don't do it and get away with it?' Gerry asked curiously.

'Impossible!' gasped Wayne.

'Like to bet?'

'Bookies never bet!' said Wayne scornfully. 'It's a mug's game!'

In registration on Monday morning, Gerry was the centre of attention.

'I feel quietly confident,' he told Tim. 'I've been in training all over the weekend and I think I'm fully prepared.'

'I couldn't eat this morning!' Tim confessed. 'I kept on thinking about what Mr Haggerty was going to do to you. It put me off my breakfast!'

'I had porridge, kippers and toast!' said Gerry nonchalantly. 'I got a couple of Mars bars down on the way to school as well!'

'No point dying on an empty stomach, I suppose!' said Tim.

Gerry smiled enigmatically.

The air in the French room was electric. The spectators took their seats and a buzz of excitement went around as Gerry Atkins, one of the contenders, took his place at the back of the class. The buzz died to an expectant silence as Mr Haggerty entered and the crowd prepared themselves for a no-holds-barred contest.

'Take out your exercise books and turn to your homework!' commanded Mr Haggerty.

In the ensuing shuffle, Gerry's arm lifted into the air. 'Please, sir, may I leave the room, sir!' he whispered desperately.

'No you may not, Atkins! Too much for you, eh, laddie?' sneered Mr Haggerty. 'Lost the stomach for it? Open that exercise book.'

'But . . . sir . . .'

'Do as you're told!' bawled Mr Haggerty.

Gerry opened his French book on the table. 'Sir . . .' he whimpered.

'It's no use being pathetic!' boomed Mr Haggerty, advancing. 'There's no escape this time, is there, laddie? I've got you right—'

Gerry was sick—gloriously and spectacularly sick—all over his French book.

The next morning, Mr Haggerty sent for Gerry during registration and met him in the French Department Office.

'All right, Atkins!' he sighed. 'You win. I want to call a truce.'

'Sir?' said Gerry innocently.

'We'll forget about the homeworks you owe me, but as of this Friday, you'll do your French like everybody else, or I'll take you to the Headmaster. Is that clear?'

'Yes, sir.'

Mr Haggerty handed over a new exercise book. 'No more excuses, Atkins?'

'No, sir!'

'Right!' smiled Mr Haggerty. 'When you get back to your form base, send Wayne Armitage over to me. I want to collect my winnings.'

'Winnings, sir?' frowned Gerry.

'Yes,' said Mr Haggerty. 'I bet 2p that you'd get away with it yesterday. Wayne offered odds of a hundred-to-one. He owes me two pounds.'

Digging for Trouble

Marian Abbey

To whoever finds this:

I might not get to the end of this story. I might get murdered first. It all depends if Someone gets back from school before I get to the end. So I'm going to write it down quickly, OK? So that you can find it. I want someone to know what happened to me, Sam.

I hope you can read this. It's difficult, writing under here. But it seems the safest place. Trouble is, I can't hear things very well here. So it's not that safe. I need to know when the front door opens and the yelling, bag-waving terror of Doherty Road runs up the stairs and . . .

I'm wasting time, aren't I? Sorry.

It started this morning. First day back at school and you could see Dad was itching to get rid of us. He didn't exactly hang out the flags or kick us out of the front door, but I saw his reflection in the kitchen window and he was grinning. Great big grin. Almost rubbing his hands to get us out so that he could go back to his jewellery.

Dad and his jewellery. He makes it. (I've put that in just in case it's not Dad who finds this.) You'd think that someone who spends all day with tiny little fiddly things would be more careful. Wouldn't lose things? Would have a better idea of colour? Well, you'd be wrong, because . . .

Sorry. Back to the story.

First day back at school, and when we got there the teachers were walking around like zombies. Another year of having to put up with us lot. They all looked shellshocked. You know the look—it's as pleased as your parents' look on Christmas morning when you jump on their stomachs to wake them up and they groan and say something like 'it's only five o'clock, go away'. Anyway, Mrs French, our class teacher, looked like she wanted to say 'go away', but knew she couldn't. So she went all original (I don't think) and got us writing. Anything to keep us quiet.

'Write about something that happened during the holidays,' she said. We all groaned, but she pretended not to notice.

'What sort of thing, Miss?' Freddie asked. He's always asking stupid questions.

'Oh, anything. I know, Freddie . . .' Mrs F suddenly seemed a bit brighter. '. . . tell me about something frightening—or funny.'

Well, that was that. I knew I wouldn't be able to write anything at all. Because nothing had happened during the summer. It wasn't like Alix, who went camping and woke the next morning to find there was a bull in the field. I didn't have a baby sister like Jim, who pulled down all the bags of sugar in Sainsbury's when their mother wasn't looking.

I looked at the blank paper and it looked back at me.

Everyone else was scribbling away.

'Sam . . .'

I glanced up. Mrs French was frowning. Warning. Better write something.

Something frightening. Something funny. On holiday.

And then I remembered. A doddle. Easy peasy. Watch me write!

There I was, scribbling away like everyone else. Something that happened. Yes! I'd even finish writing before break.

I thought I was writing a story.

I didn't realize it was my death warrant.

I wrote all about how we went on holiday, to the seaside. And how my parents thought up a Great Beach Game to keep my sister happy. The game was Bury The Yellow Dolly. My sister's best dolly. My sister's very-favourite, mustn't-ever-lose, can't-get-to-sleep-without-it yellow dolly.

Mum and Dad buried the dolly, and my sister dug it up, giggling. They buried it again and she found it, one yellow leg sticking out of the yellow sand. They buried it, deeper, and she scrabbled around for a bit and finally found it, laughing.

Then my daft mum and dad went and buried the thing even deeper the next time. And they never, ever, found it again.

You wouldn't think you could lose something on a beach if you knew where you'd buried it, would you? But take it from me, you can. Very easily. Try it, next time you go to the seaside. But don't bury anything you care about.

My sister dug around, and couldn't find her doll. 'I'll help,' said Dad, casual-like. He started moving the sand aside, slowly at first, then faster and faster. Like a mole, or something trying to swim into the sand. Dad's face changed—you should have seen it. It went pink, then white, then a sort of grey colour. And when Mum realized what had happened she joined in too. Panic wasn't the word.

'We've got to find it,' she panted. 'We've *got* to.'

But they didn't.

I tried to help, but it was no good. I think the beach is just a thin layer of sand on top that looks as if it stays still, but underneath is a moving load of quicksand that takes things away on a conveyor belt and moves them around the beach.

My sister stopped giggling. She went very quiet, and then she started to cry. She howled and howled.

We went back to the hotel, and she was crying.

We had tea, and she was crying more.

Mum and Dad tried to put her to bed, and she was still howling.

That evening, Mum and Dad went back to the beach. They spent the whole night digging in the sand. They said it was really embarrassing. People kept walking along the road, calling down:

'Hey, aren't you two a bit old for that?'

'The worms'll be down towards the water, din ye know?'

'The sun's gone in, if you hadn't noticed.'

They came back with very bad tempers but no doll.

My sister cried for the rest of the holiday. The hotel got really fed up.

They moved our table into another room, because it was putting people off their breakfast. My sister wouldn't go to bed, and every night Mum and Dad had to walk her up and down until she went to sleep.

The next day they went out and bought her another doll, but it wasn't Yellow Dolly so it didn't count. And then she realized that if she kept crying, she'd keep getting presents. So my sister cried every day for a week, and went home with four dolls, a panda, and a dead finger which glowed in the dark.

Now, I don't usually write things in class. And I've never written anything good. So it never occurred to me what could happen to my story.

After lunch, I went back into school and found a load of people gathered around the notice board, giggling and nudging each other. I went over and saw something surprising—my own writing staring back at me. I felt quite good, until I saw the heading. And noticed that the others had gone quiet and were watching me carefully.

I saw the story about my sister. Crying. For a dolly. Underneath a banner which said:

THIS SUMMER HOLIDAY

John pulled my sleeve. 'Her class went out and bought her a doll at lunchtime.'

Emma whispered, 'Joanne gave her a handkerchief in case she needed it to blow her nose.'

Someone else said, 'Jake Einsom told her to stop crying and she knocked him over.'

My life flashed in front of me.

I haven't told you about my sister, have I? She's called Janet at home, and Big Jan at school. I come up to her left shoulder. Her right shoulder's higher because of all the training she does for discus-throwing. And brother-throwing.

I might be older than her, but I'm smaller. A lot smaller. I haven't been the same size as her since the beach holiday. And that was seven years ago.

Was that the front door? It's difficult to tell, and I don't want to check, just in case.

It's very stuffy here. And cramped. But I like it.

I think I'll stay here for ever and ever.

The One that Got Away

JAN MARK

'And what have we to remember to bring tomorrow?' Mrs Cooper asked, at half past three. Malcolm, sitting near the back, wondered why she said 'we'. *She* wasn't going to bring anything.

'Something interesting, Mrs Cooper,' said everyone else, all together.

'And what are we going to do then?'

'Stand up and talk about it, Mrs Cooper.'

'So don't forget. All right. Chairs on tables. Goodbye, Class Four.'

'Goodbye, Mrs Cooper. Goodbye, everybody.'

It all came out ever so slow, like saying prayers in assembly. 'Amen,' said Malcolm, very quietly. Class Four put its chairs on the tables, collected its coats and went home, talking about all the interesting things it would bring into school tomorrow.

Malcolm walked by himself. Mrs Cooper had first told them to find something interesting on Monday. Now it was Thursday and still he had not come up with any bright ideas. There were plenty of things that he found interesting, but the trouble was, they never seemed to interest anyone else. Last time this had happened he had brought along his favourite stone and shown it to the class.

'Very nice, Malcolm,' Mrs Cooper had said. 'Now tell us what's interesting about it.' He hadn't known what to say. Surely anyone looking at the stone could see how interesting it was.

Mary was going to bring her gerbil. James, Sarah, and William had loudly discussed rare shells and fossils, and the only spider in the world with five legs.

'It can't be a spider then,' said David, who was eavesdropping.

'It had an accident,' William said.

Isobel intended to bring her pocket calculator and show them how it could write her name by punching in 738051 and turning it upside down. She did this every time, but it still looked interesting.

Malcolm could think of nothing.

When he reached home he went up to his bedroom and looked at the shelf where he kept important things; his twig that looked like a stick insect, his marble that looked like a glass eye, the penny with a hole in it and the Siamese-twin jelly-babies, one red, one green and stuck together, back to back. He noticed that they were now stuck to the shelf, too. His stone had once been there as well, but after Class Four had said it was boring he had put it back in the garden. He still went to see it sometimes.

What he really needed was something that could move about, like Mary's gerbil or William's five-legged spider. He sat down on his bed and began to think.

On Friday, after assembly, Class Four began to be interesting. Mary kicked off with the gerbil that whirred round its cage like a hairy balloon with the air escaping. Then they saw William's lame spider, James's fossil, Jason's collection of snail shells stuck one on top of the other like the leaning tower of Pisa, and David's bottled conkers that he had kept in an air-tight jar for three years. They were still as glossy as new shoes.

Then it was Malcolm's turn. He went up to the front and held out a matchbox. He had chosen it very carefully. It was the kind with the same label top and bottom so that when you opened it you could never be sure that it was the right way up and all the matches fell out. Malcolm opened it upside down and jumped. Mrs Cooper jumped too. Malcolm threw himself down on hands and knees and looked under her desk.

'What's the matter?' Mrs Cooper said.

'It's fallen out!' Malcolm cried.

'What is it?' Mrs Cooper said, edging away.

'I don't know — it's got six legs and sharp knees . . . and sort of frilly ginger eyebrows on stalks —' He pounced. 'There it goes.'

'Where?'

'Missed it,' said Malcolm. 'It's running under your chair, Mary.'

Mary squeaked and climbed onto the table because she thought that was the right way to behave when creepy-crawlies were about.

'I see it!' Jason yelled, and jumped up and down. David threw a book in the direction that Jason was pointing and James began beating the floor with a rolled-up comic.

'I got it — I killed it,' he shouted.

'It's crawling up the curtains,' Sarah said and Mrs Cooper, who was standing by the curtains, moved rapidly away from them.

'It's over by the door,' Mary shrieked, and several people ran to head it off. Chairs were overturned.

Malcolm stood by Mrs Cooper's desk with his matchbox. His contribution was definitely the most interesting thing that anyone had seen that morning. He was only sorry that he hadn't seen it himself.

Sick as a Parrot

MICHAELA MORGAN

The Sullivans are such a sensible family. Granny Sullivan sweeps and sorts. 'A place for everything and everything in its own place,' she says.

Mum dusts and polishes. 'Spick and span, clean and shiny,' she says.

And then there's Dad. He likes to tidy and organize. 'Soon have everything sorted,' he says. 'Neat and tidy. Clean as a whistle.'

Even the twins, Jake and Kate, are sensible. They have never lost a single sock in their lives and they keep their toys in alphabetical order. A for Action man, B for Barbie, C for Cluedo right down to X for xylophone.

So that Tuesday in June was a bit of a shock for them.

'I do not believe it!' said Dad. 'I can't find a single spoon.' He was getting a bit cross. His Rice Krispies were turning into Rice Soggies and he was considering trying to eat them with a fork.

'Has someone moved my best silver ear-rings?' shouted Mum. 'I can't find them anywhere!'

'Where's my collection of bottle tops?' moaned Jake.

'And where's my jar of five pences?' groaned Kate.

'And what about my silver-backed hairbrush,' said Gran. 'Who's taken that?'

'Burglar perhaps,' said Dad. 'But what sort of a burglar takes silver spoons and bottle tops and leaves the video, the telly, and the computer?'

'Magpie perhaps?' suggested Mum.

'Pirate actually,' said a deep voice. 'And afore ye start a-bellowing and a-billowing you can have it all back if you just let me go.'

'*Let me go! Let me go!*' squawked another voice.

The voices were coming from the curtains, which had a suspicious pirate-shaped bulge in them.

At the bottom of the curtains one salt-encrusted boot peeped out. Towards the top of the curtains was a pointy beak shape.

'Hmmm . . . suspicious,' said Dad.

Mum just tutted and pulled the curtains back.

'Just what do you think you're doing?' she demanded.

There, with his wooden leg out of the open window, was a big, burly, bearded pirate.

'Short Bob Silver's the name,' the pirate said, smiling weakly. 'Pleased to meet you.' He offered to shake his hook with Gran. She just sniffed. He didn't look their sort of person at all. He was not neat and tidy in the least. He seemed to have mislaid several bits of his body rather carelessly (a hand, a leg, and an eye were obviously lacking). He did not look sensible at all.

He had a dusty patch on one eye, a scruffy, balding parrot on one shoulder, and a fierce dog holding on to his one good leg. The dog was Rover, the Sullivan family pet. He had his teeth stuck into the pirate's trouser leg and he wasn't letting go.

'Good dog, Rover,' said Dad. 'You've got him trapped.'

'Erm . . . I don't suppose you could persuade him to let go of my leg, could you?' asked the pirate.

'Give me my five pences back first,' said Kate fiercely.

'And my bottle tops,' said Jake.

'And take my ear-rings off at once,' said Mum. 'You look ridiculous.'

'You can have it all back,' growled the pirate.

'*All back,*' echoed the parrot.

'Just let me go!'

'*Lemme go!*' the bird agreed.

So the Sullivan family took all their stuff back and told Rover to let go. But he didn't. He wouldn't. He couldn't.

'Oh, the poor thing! He's got his teeth stuck in your trousers,' said Kate.

'We'll have to cut him free.'

Gran went off to get her sewing scissors.

The pirate hopped and limped over to the sofa, dragging his leg, and the dog, behind him.

'Poor Rover,' said Jake, 'soon have you free.'

'Poor Rover!' snorted the pirate. 'What about poor me?'

'You deserve it,' said Dad, sternly. 'You're a disgrace, stealing other people's belongings.'

'It was just a few pieces of silver,' said the pirate.

'*Pieces of silver*,' echoed the parrot.

'I was desperate,' said the pirate.

'*Desperate!*' agreed the parrot.

'It was for my poor parrot.'

'*Poor parrot . . .*' sighed the bird.

'My poor poorly parrot needs help and I need money to pay the vet.'

'*Pay the vet! Pay the vet!*' the bedraggled bird insisted.

'I'm desperate to buy a cure for my faithful feathered friend 'ere. This parrot is very sick.'

'*Sick*,' said the parrot and he sighed.

'He does look a bit green,' said Kate.

'He went off his food,' said the pirate.

'*Food!*' said the parrot.

'But I could tell he was still hungry.'

'*Still hungry . . .*'

'He was fading away.'

'*Fading away . . .*'

'Poor thing,' said Kate.

'*Poor thing*,' the parrot agreed and put his head under his wing.

'What have you been feeding him?' asked Mum.

'The usual,' said Short Bob. 'Scraps o' this and scraps o' that. Oh, and I've been giving 'im this special medicine that I still owe the vet for.'

Jake sniffed the medicine. It was thick and green and gloppy like the contents of a particularly unpleasant handkerchief. It smelt like old socks, raw liver, and brussels sprouts.

'Yuck!' said Jake.

'*YUCK!*' agreed the parrot.

Gran was peering at the parrot. 'It's half starved, poor thing,' she said. 'I know about birds. They need to eat grain and seed or else they go . . .'

'*Nuts?*' suggested the parrot.

'Can't bear to see a poor helpless creature suffering,' said Gran. 'Leave that parrot with me. I'll soon have him sorted.'

And that's how a sensible family like the Sullivans came to have a parrot living in their bathroom. (Gran thought the steam and heat would perk it up.)

They also ended up with a pirate in the attic.

'I love that bird,' Short Bob had said. 'I've loved him since he was an egg. If he's staying, so am I.'

So he did.

The pirate soon made himself at home.

He made a few things for his room, did a bit of painting and decorating, helped with the washing and the shopping, and was particularly good at cleaning and babysitting.

He was very good with the baby. He'd rock it in a hammock, tell it tall tales, and sing sea shanties. He even liked changing nappies.

What shall we do with a dirty nappy?
What shall we do with a dirty nappy?
What shall we do with a dirty nappy?
Early in the morning?

Peel it off and stuff it in a bucket
Peel it off and stuff it in a bucket
Peel it off and stuff it in a bucket
Early in the morning.

Clean 'im up and dry 'im nicely
Clean 'im up and dry 'im nicely
Clean 'im up and dry 'im nicely
Early in the morning.

'*Yo ho ho and powder his bum!*' added the parrot.

'I don't know how we ever managed without him,' said the Sullivans. They'd found that living with a rough tough type can be a rather refreshing experience. After only a few days the sensible Sullivans were climbing and clambering and swinging and singing and yo ho hoing better than Short Bob.

'I feel years younger!' whooped Gran as she swung across the living room. 'This pirate life's a proper tonic!'

And Short Bob was becoming neater and tidier and more sensible by the minute. Now he had a well brushed beard, gleaming teeth, and a clean hanky. Not to mention a shiny polished wooden leg, a sparkling hook, and clean underpants.

The only problem was the parrot. It had perked up a bit but it was still looking seedy. It was losing its feathers one by one and spent most of the day dozing in the corner, just waking from time to time to mutter something rude and then nod off again.

'We've tried everything,' sighed Mum.

'If we don't cure it soon,' said Jake, 'it will be completely bald and then it won't be able to fly.' He knew all about parrots now. He'd borrowed every book he could find in the library. A picture of a featherless parrot had filled him with horror. 'We can't let this poor parrot end up like that,' he moaned.

But what could they do?

They'd tried giving it healthy food. The parrot would just look at it and sigh.

They'd tried teaching it keep-fit exercises. The parrot wouldn't even try.

They'd kept it in a hot-and-steamy-rain-forest-type-place (the bathroom). The parrot just got damp.

Short Bob would sing to it and tickle it and tell it tall tales to cheer it up—but nothing worked. As he watched his faithful friend fading away, great big blobby tears would creep down Short Bob's hairy cheek. They splashed on to the parrot, who just sat slumped and still, getting even damper.

One afternoon, however, things looked up. Short Bob had moved some of his belongings into the Sullivans' house and what a mess they were! Dusty, tattered, untidy! In no order at all! The Sullivan family couldn't wait to get tidying and dusting and polishing and sorting it all out into a ship-shape and sensible fashion.

One by one, the pirate's long lost belongings were turned up by Gran's relentless tidying and organizing.

'Well, what do you know, my spare leg!' said Bob. 'That will come in handy! And what's that? My winter vest! And what a lot of papers!'

There were a lot of papers. There were old bus tickets, swimming certificates, vet's bills (there were lots of those), some very interesting treasure maps, recipes and fashion tips, and this:

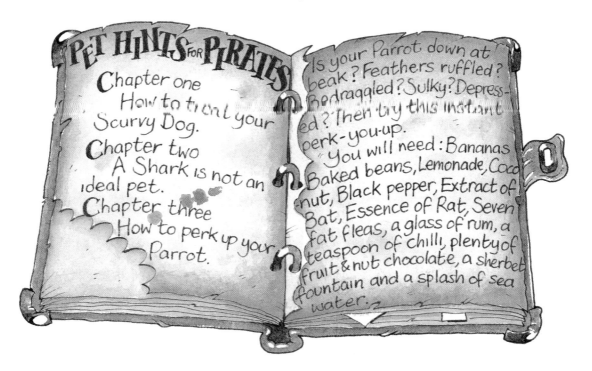

PET HINTS FOR PIRATES

Chapter one
  How to treat your
Scurvy Dog.
Chapter two
  A Shark is not an
ideal pet.
Chapter three
  How to perk up your
  Parrot.

Is your Parrot down at beak? Feathers ruffled? Bedraggled? Sulky? Depressed? Then try this instant perk-you-up.
  You will need: Bananas Baked beans, Lemonade, Coconut, Black pepper, Extract of Bat, Essence of Rat, Seven fat fleas, a glass of rum, a teaspoon of chilli, plenty of fruit & nut chocolate, a sherbet fountain and a splash of sea water.

'Ooh, aar!' said Short Bob. 'Some o' these papers must belong to my grandaddy or my great-grandaddy or my great-great-great-grandaddy. Or my great-great-great-great-great . . .'

'No one's that great,' said Gran crisply. 'I think we should try this out. See if it works. We'll need a guinea pig.'

'But I 'aven't got no guinea pig,' sighed the sailor. 'All I's got is this 'ere bird.'

'We'll explain it to you later, dear,' said Gran. 'Right now I've got some shopping to do. I'm off.'

'*I'm off,*' the parrot agreed.

In no time at all (considering how difficult it is to find extract of bat in Tesco's) Kate, Jake, and Gran were holding a bowl full of interesting titbits in front of the jaded parrot.

'*Rats!*' it said.

'Try a bit,' urged Kate, 'we've all worked hard on this. We're all . . .'

'*Bananas?*' suggested the parrot.

'Now you just be sensible, dear, and have a beak of this,' said Gran, offering the coconut.

'*I should coco,*' sulked the parrot.

Kate forced some sherbet and pepper into the parrot's unwilling beak.

Jake squashed in some baked beans, lemonade, and other bits. 'Come on,' he said. 'We're just . . .'

'*Bats!*' muttered the parrot through clenched beak.

'Stand back,' said Dad. 'Time for the seawater.' He aimed a bucketful of freezing saltwater at the miserable bird.

'Stand well back now,' shouted Gran. And just as well. Because the parrot started to perk up.

First he opened one bleary eye and sighed in the usual way.

Then he hiccuped and jumped.

He began to fizz and pop.

One particularly large pop and he'd fallen beak first into the rest of the bowl. He lay there opening and closing his beak and blinking.

Then '*Mmmm?*' said the parrot and '*Rum?*' said the parrot. He sat up straight and burped. '*Yum!*' said the parrot. A beakful of fruit and nut chocolate and '*Chocs away!*' he squawked and fairly whizzed around the room. Hiccuping and burping and making little popping noises that embarrassed even him, he whirled around flapping and squawking.

His feathers shone. His beak glowed.

'*Supersonic!*' shrieked the parrot as he looped the loop. '*What a tonic!*' and he dive-bombed back into the bowl screeching and squawking, singing and talking. Why, he even started to tap dance!

'Well, that seems to have done the trick,' said Gran, coming in with tea and chocolate cake. 'I'm sure your vet would buy a recipe like that. I reckon your bill's paid.'

'*Bill's paid! Bill's paid!*' whooped the parrot. He'd never liked being in debt.

''Is name's Jim not Bill,' said the pirate, 'but I reckon you do be right. If 'e don't take this 'ere Parrot Perk You Up as payment my name's not Short Bob. Which it is,' he added rather pointlessly.

'*Parrot power!*' squawked the parrot who was now full of beans, not to mention fruit and nut chocolate, lemonade and sherbet. He perched on Gran's head. '*Who's a pretty girl then?*' he enquired.

Gran blushed. 'Who'd like a bit of chocolate cake, then?' she asked.

'Ooh, arr!' said Short Bob. 'I do be wantin' a bit. I do be . . .'

'*Do be do be do,*' sang the parrot.

'Aye,' continued the pirate. 'I do be wantin' a bit of that there cake and then I do be wantin' . . . to see the sea again. I reckon a bit o' seawater would do us all good! Who'd like a trip in my boat, then?'

'Ooh, arr!' said all the Sullivans. 'Yes, please!'

'All aboard, then!' said the pirate. 'Set sail! There be seas to be sailed and fun to be had. All aboard!'

'*All aboard!*' said the parrot and with one happy burp he flapped his shiny, many-coloured wings, took flight and led the way.

Like Dog, Like Dad

W. K. McNeil

A man was prowling around his house and he got hungry. His wife was off somewhere—might have been a club meeting; she'd gone somewhere. He was hungry; looking around for something to eat and happened to find a biscuit lying on the radiator. Some kind of biscuit! He didn't know what kind it was; it was just a biscuit. He was hungry. He tried it and he liked it. He ate it and then after his wife got home he said to her, 'What kind of biscuit was that on the radiator?'

'Why do you ask?' she replied. 'What it was was one of the dog biscuits.'

'Well now, I was hungry and I didn't know what kind of biscuit it was and I thought I'd try it and I did and it was good.'

'It was a dog biscuit and you shouldn't have eaten it.'

'Well, I was hungry and I didn't know what kind of biscuit it was and I thought I'd try it and I did and it was good.'

'Oh now, you'd better not do that,' she replied.

'Now, I want some more of them and when you do your shopping get some more dog biscuits.'

'Well, then, if that is what you want.'

So the next time she went marketing she bought just twice as many dog biscuits as she was in the habit of buying. And the clerk who had watched her in her buying for quite a while noted she was buying twice as many dog biscuits. She'd always bought the same amount every time.

'Buying twice as many?' the employee said. 'I see you're buying twice as many dog biscuits. Have you got another dog?'

'No, I don't have another dog. It's just that my husband happened to get hold of a dog biscuit the other day and he didn't know what it was. He ate it and he was hungry and he ate it. I wasn't at home. He ate it; he was hungry so he ate it. And when I came home he asked me what kind it was and I told him. He said he wanted some more of them, so that is why I'm buying twice as many.'

'Now,' the clerk said, 'you better not encourage him to eat those dog biscuits, they might make him sick. They might not be good for him.' But she went ahead and got them anyway.

She went ahead getting them regularly for quite a little spell. Then finally, she went in to do her shopping and just got her old original number that she'd got when she was just feeding the dog. The clerk again observed the different size order. 'You're only getting the amount you used to get when you were only buying for your dog? What is the matter? Is your husband getting tired of dog biscuits and not wanting any more?'

'Oh, it's not that! My husband is dead. My husband is dead.'

'I'm sorry to hear that, but I warned you. I told you they might make him sick. They might hurt him.'

'Oh, no, no they didn't. He got killed!'

'Got killed? How?'

'Chasing cars,' she replied.

Sniff, Miss Morris, and a Bit of Cuckoo Spit

IAN WHYBROW

I don't think my sister Sal would have bitten my finger quite so hard if I hadn't tried to get the worm out of her mouth. Normally I wouldn't have bothered but this was one of *mine*. I had collected a number of them in a shoebox which I had carefully *placed* (not left lying around) near the lettuces by the back fence in the garden. I knew it was one of mine because it was encased in a particularly rich black mud that I had created to give them the sense that they were on holiday, rather than the subjects of a scientific investigation. I had had one or two tips from Miss Salt in Biology about how hermaphrodites breed, but I wanted to see for myself how things worked out when you put them together.

'Dop it!' screamed Sal, kicking out as I tried to lever her mouth open with my finger and thumb.

'Give it to me!' I said firmly. 'You eat your own.'

'I found it!' she insisted through tightly clenched teeth. From somewhere deep down in her dungarees, she worked up a shriek. Her mouth was full of worm so the shriek had to come out through her nostrils. Even so, I reckon it was still piercing enough to interfere with television reception. Suddenly I heard somebody else screaming along with her. It was me. She'd practically bitten my index finger in half.

It must have been this double scream that got Sniff away from his usual post by the front gate. He likes to hide behind it until people go by and then he throws himself against the railings at the top so that they drop their shopping or fall off their bikes. Today, I had noticed him happily occupied, lying in

a shallow puddle of water Dad had made when he washed the car. Sniff was amusing himself with what looked to me from a distance like a tea-bag. He was knocking it about with his nose and paws, then tossing it up in the air and catching it in his jaws. Anyway, he came charging down the side-passage and when he saw me struggling with Sal, trying to get my bitten finger out of her mouth, he immediately rushed back a few feet, gathered up his tea-bag again and then came bounding up to us on the lawn, woofing hysterically, yiking like locked brakes and trying to squeeze his tea-bag in between us.

It was not my day at all. First my sister ate one of my best worms. Then she sank her choppers into my finger so hard she made it bleed. Finally, Sniff bounced at me, caught me off-balance and I slipped and smacked my head on the ground.

I was dizzy for a second, but I could tell Sniff was still pounding about, trying to play, because he made little charging, growling runs at me as I lay on the grass and every now and then he butted me in the ribs with his nose or with a big paw. As I slowly opened my eyes, I focused on the bedroom window of the house next door. There, behind the net curtains, I could clearly see the pale face of Miss Morris, her bulging eyes registering total horror.

Dad says he reckons Miss Morris was brought up in India and had a nanny. I think this is quite likely because there are a lot of things she doesn't seem to know about. For one thing, she doesn't know much about dogs or fights. If you've ever been one of a crowd watching a nice little scrap, and everybody is shouting 'Fight! Fight!', you'll know that you can't stand there long without giving the kid next to you a bit of a rough-up too. You know, your arms sort of *automatically* go round his neck and then you have a roll round and a good bit of friendly duffing up. Poor old Miss Morris. She was probably never *allowed* to enjoy a good scrap—so how could she work out for herself that Sniff had got into the fight between Sal and me for the doggy equivalent of a laugh? What she thought she saw from her upstairs window was

the brutal attack by a mad and rather
untidy Hound of the Baskervilles on
two defenceless young kiddiwinks who
were so terrified that they were
clinging together for support.

Anyway, I was sitting up, seeing how
many drops of blood I could squeeze
from the toothmarks in my injured
finger, when Miss Morris arrived in the
garden. She looked even more wild-
eyed than usual and was waving a hefty
great walking-stick over her head. She
had a great collection of sticks in an
umbrella stand in her hall. I saw it once
through her letterbox when she was
out.

'Get back, you brute!' she shouted.
'Leave! Leave!'

Sniff was delighted to carry on with
the game. He took a flying leap and
grabbed Miss Morris's raised walking-
stick and then he was off. He charged
round the garden with it, doing a fair bit
of damage, first to the sunflowers, then
to the runner beans, pausing now and
then to give the walking-stick a shake in
case there was any life left in it. He got
it caught up in the strings supporting
the tomato-plants and soon he was
dragging a couple of their bamboo canes
with him into the flower-bed. He
ploughed in among the chrysanthe-

mums, flattening most of them and scattering their petals about like coloured snow. When he'd done two or three lunatic circuits, he returned to give Miss Morris a chance to grab the stick and a really thorough bumping and sniffling at the same time, just to show how grateful he was to her for being such a surprisingly good sport.

Miss Morris's reaction to this was to throw her arms in a protective knot across her ears and eyes and to bend double. Personally, I would never have tried anything like that with Sniff. He'd had a couple of nasty experiences with hedgehogs in the garden, so he'd learned that in some cases the softly-softly approach was less painful. But just because he wasn't going to be rough, it didn't mean that he wasn't going to do something rude. He dropped the walking-stick and crouched down. It was lucky that my mind had now cleared completely since the crack to my head, and that I was able to figure out what his next move would be. He was going to try to uncurl her by poking his powerful nose up under that tempting, tweed-skirted bottom. Something told me that Miss Morris would not see the funny side of this and, just in time, I distracted him by shaking the walking-stick under his chin. He immediately grabbed it between his teeth and worried it

fiercely for a moment or two—until he suddenly caught sight of his tea-bag and decided that it was more interesting. He pounced on it and shook it like a rat.

All this gave Miss Morris the opportunity to uncurl herself of her own accord, while I did my best to sit on what I could get hold of of the panting, rasping Sniffy-Boy. Sal thought this was dead funny and sat gurgling with laughter while mud and chewed worm dribbled on to her T-shirt. Perhaps because part of what I had been sitting on was head (it was always difficult to tell with Sniff), he was in need of a bit of air when I got off him. That was why he was kicking out so wildly, I suppose. Still, it didn't explain his spluttering and coughing and the litres of white froth coming out of his mouth.

Have you ever seen one of those films where the eyes in a painting move as the hero creeps among the suits of armour towards the secret passage? That was how Miss Morris's eyes moved in her drained and frozen face as they took in the foaming jaws of Sniff and then the smears of blood on my thumb and forefinger.

'He's bitten you!' she whispered. 'He's drawn blood! And look at his mouth . . .!' she mouthed, as though she didn't want Sniff to hear. Then she added, '. . . dear.'

Dear, eh? This was laying it on a bit thick. But then I thought—aha! She's trying to soften me up so that I'll tell her where Mum is. Cunning, eh? Because when you tell people like Miss Morris where your mum is, they go and tell them about something you've been up to and then you get into trouble for it. I had to get the old brain working quickly. What had I done recently that she wanted to get me for? Looking through her letterbox, maybe? Anyway, I had to do some quick thinking.

'She's—er—not here,' I said. I thought that was pretty good on the spur of the moment because she obviously *wasn't*. I didn't want to be more precise and say that she had gone to the library because I felt that Miss Morris might hang around and boss us about. Anyhow, Dad was looking after us—except that he was in the garage— but I certainly wasn't going to mention it to Miss Morris. I happened to know that he was stripping down the carburettor on the car, which is a dead fiddly job, and I know he doesn't like to be disturbed while he's concentrating.

'Dreadful,' she said. 'How dreadful.' She seemed uncertain what to do next but suddenly she took a deep breath. She'd decided something. 'Don't worry,' she said with great dignity, in spite of the fact that something had come undone in her hair and she was looking a bit freaky. 'Don't worry. I shan't abandon you. *I* shall be no more than a few minutes.'

At that, she left the garden at a speed that startled Sniff so much that he leapt to his feet and scrambled towards her. Luckily, I caught him by the tail and, before he got his great paws properly untangled, managed to hang on to him while, with a whimper and an extra little spurt, Miss Morris sprinted down the side-passage in what I should think was a record-breaking time. I gave my injured finger a soothing suck.

'What dat?' asked Sal, pointing at Sniff who was frantically trying to scrape froth from round his head with his front legs.

'Cuckoo-spit,' I said, confidently. 'He probably ate some when he dived into the hedge just now.'

'What tootoo pit?' Sal enquired. I was going to flash my knowledge at her. We'd done frog-hoppers in Biology. I was trying to work out a way of explaining to her how the nymphs of certain insects, and particularly the frog-hopper, protect themselves by

making little frothy nests among the leaves, when it occurred to me that it might not be the right time of the year. Then something told me that she wasn't really interested in cuckoo-spit, because she was crawling at full speed towards my worm-box again. And as I dashed off to stop her messing about with my experiment, something else occurred to me. The ragged tea-bag that lay on the lawn by the still-frothing Sniff was not in fact a tea-bag at all. It was actually an empty sachet of Turtle Wax car shampoo.

'Aha!' I said out loud. Another case wrapped up by the great Sherlock Moore!

When Mum got home from the library, she stood in the garden as if she was visiting some ruin and trying to figure out where everything was when it was all there. I think she was quite pleased when she came through the front door with her books and saw the vase of chrysanthemums on the hall table. But when she came through into the kitchen and saw that there were another six vases full and some others with sunflowers, tomato-plants and runner beans in, you could tell she thought this was a bit of a bummer.

'But why did you *do* this, guys?' she said, looking hopelessly round the garden. I could tell this was serious and

that she was beginning to think she had failed as a Mother. (I had heard her getting uptight about this before, when she and Dad were talking about how Sal kept wetting her knickers—but don't ask me what that had to do with failing as a mother.) Anyhow, I decided to explain how Miss Morris had just wandered in and got the dog going.

'How do you mean, Ben, "*got the dog going*"?'

'He too excited,' put in Sal, who had a lot of experience of being Too Excited.

'Miss Morris came in and gave him a stick,' I explained. 'And that sort of wound him up.'

'Miss Morris? Miss Morris came in? Miss Morris never comes in. She hardly speaks to us. Why would she want to come into our garden?'

'She lookin' for you,' said Sal.

'Yes,' I said. 'I told her you weren't here and then she said "How dreadful" or something and not to worry, she'd be back.'

Mum blushed. One second she was looking pale and the next she was all red. She snatched up Sal and cuddled her. 'But I was only gone for twenty minutes. I told you where I was going, and Dad knew where I was. I was only down the road at the library, wasn't I? I offered to take you but you said you preferred to stay and look after Sniff. Where is he, by the way? And where's Dad?'

'In the garage,' I said.

'With Radio 3 blaring away, I expect,' said Mum, angrily.

'Miff hidin',' Sal said.

'Why is Sniff hiding, Ben?'

'Ben naughty!' Sal said. 'He squirt Miff wid da hose-pie. Miff all wet.'

At this moment, the Whee-whee-whee! and the Dah-da, Dah-da! that had been going on in the background became very loud and close. There was a squeal of brakes, doors slammed, and Sniff, who, since I had hosed him down, had gone to hide in the house somewhere, suddenly came zooming out of the back door and charged down the side-passage to see what was going on out in the road. Seconds later, he was charging back. He threw himself down on the lawn behind Mum where she was standing, still clutching Sal, and hid his head up her dress.

We all stood dead still. I was listening so hard I could hear whistling in my

ears—and then we heard the slow crunching of gravel under boots.

The first thing that came into sight was a large, trembling net. When he saw it, Sniff began to shake violently and tried to hide himself further under Mum's skirt.

'Now don't panic, madam,' came the nervous voice of the policeman from behind the folds of the net.

'Where's the dog? Can you see it yet?' hissed a deeper voice from behind him.

'Can't see it yet, Sarge,' said the policeman. 'Only the woman and the kids.'

'We'll soon have you safe, madam,' confided the voice of the hidden Sergeant. 'We've got an ambulance for the boy and PC Fuller will—er—see to the dog. Everything's just fine. Just take your time and bring the kiddies round to the front of the house . . .'

'You can't take them away from me,' wailed Mum. 'I didn't *leave* them. I was

only gone for twenty minutes. And anyway, their dad was here all the time. I just went to the library. We wouldn't leave them alone, honestly. You see, Ben was here to keep an eye on my little girl, and he's a very sensible boy, so what was the harm in . . . I mean, they didn't want to come . . . It was only this once . . . We're really careful about things like that. I mean, we never *neglect* them or anything . . . Can't you just leave them here with me . . . and their dad? I don't know what Miss Morris has told you but . . . I only went to the library . . .'

'Never mind about libraries, madam. Be reasonable. They're not safe here, are they?' cooed the Sergeant. 'And when you come to think about it, *you're* not safe either, are you? Not with the dog in that state. Much better if you just come very quietly with us. What d'you say?'

'What do you mean? In what *state*? What's wrong with the dog?' said Mum.

'Oh my Gawd!' yelled PC Fuller, interrupting.

'What's up?' yelled the Sergeant.

'It's behind her!'

'Right, Fuller, move in! Grab the brute!' The Sergeant gave his hesitant colleague a shove and they both spilled on to the patio and into the garden.

When PC Fuller lifted his net, Sniff realized that he only wanted to play.

He dashed out from his hiding place (still looking rather damp, from the hosing down I'd given him to get the froth off, so poor Mum must have been rather uncomfortable) and, just as he had done when Miss Morris lifted her walking-stick, he jumped up, grabbed the net and tore off round the garden.

Dad arrived just in time to see Sniff pounding about the garden like some mobile windmill, demolishing most of what he hadn't already knocked down with Miss Morris's walking-stick.

There was, as they say, a certain amount of explaining to do. Quite a number of policemen, firemen, and ambulance men had to be given tea. Most of them refused rosehip and camomile and settled for Earl Grey. They sat around, sniffing at the steaming brew and raising their eyebrows appreciatively before getting out their notebooks and taking down 'the facts'. Miss Morris couldn't be persuaded to have anything and wouldn't stay long. She kept apologizing for dialling 999 under false pretences. It was the mad behaviour that had worried her and the froth round his mouth. The policemen, the ambulance men, and the firemen blew on their Earl Grey and said that it was important that the public called them if they were

suspicious because rabies was very nasty, very nasty and you never knew.

After she'd gone, they all sat round, laughing a lot, having their mugs refilled and eating all the biscuits, even the Wholemeal Carob Crunch which were expensive because they came from the health food shop. Some of the men made a note of the name and took a couple more, and I think Mum was quite pleased in a way.

They all made a fuss of Sniff which made Sal a bit jealous so she showed off and wet her knickers. I thought of asking loudly for an Elastoplast for my finger but then I thought it was definitely nobler to suffer in silence.

'He do look a bit nuts, dun he?' mused the Sergeant, giving Sniff a good scratch and winking at PC Fuller who blushed, probably thinking about his net. Sniff woofed in agreement and was rewarded by a shower of chocolate fingers from the fire brigade who wanted to give him a scratch too.

Dad didn't say much. I think he was a bit cheesed off about the flowers and the vegetables. I don't suppose he would have minded at all if Sniff had destroyed the nettles up the far end that Mum insisted on keeping to encourage butterflies. Anyway, I had an idea and asked the Chief Fireman if I could have a quick look over his fire engine. Dad cheered up when he heard this. A keen look came to his eyes. While the Chief was still nodding, I asked if Dad could have a look too.

The Chief looked a bit uncertain. 'That wouldn't put you out, would it, sir?'

'Absolutely not!' said Dad. 'I'd love to have a look round, if that's all right with you. We haven't had a close look at that particular model, have we, Ben?'

'Right, then!' said the Chief, rubbing his hands together. You could tell he didn't often get real enthusiasts like us. 'We've got one or two special features I think will interest you. All set?'

'Ready when you are!' said Dad. So that was all right.

When we came back into the kitchen, Mum had done most of the clearing up and Sal was sitting in her chair, finishing off the last of the Carob Crunch biscuits.

'You all right now, love?' said Dad. She had been a bit emotional after the Emergency Services had all kissed her goodbye.

'I'm fine, love, thanks,' she said, but her chin was wobbling a bit. 'And I think it was jolly brave of Miss Morris to come into the garden at all, actually. After all, she thought Ben and Sal were being attacked by a mad dog.'

'You're right, love,' Dad agreed. 'I think maybe we ought to give her a little something to show our appreciation.'

'What about a bunch of chrysan- themums?' I suggested, which I thought was brill but Dad didn't seem too keen.

'Ben, old son,' he said, giving me one of his over-the-top-of-the-glasses looks, 'don't push your luck.'

When I got into bed that night, I discovered where Sniff had gone to hide after I hosed him down—but I thought I'd rather keep quiet about it and put up with a bit of dampness— what with one thing and another.

I Don't Want to Wash

BEL MOONEY

'Daniel was such a good boy when he was your age,' Mum said. 'He used to go upstairs after tea to wash his face, and *without being told*!'

Kitty didn't believe it. But Dan sat at the table with a smile that said, 'Oh what a good boy am I.'

Kitty gave her big brother a dirty look. It was a very dirty look indeed because her face was all smeared with jam and soil. This was because she had run into the garden in the middle of tea and put her nose in the earth to see if she could smell the worms. She already had jam on her face and hands. So the earth stuck to the jam, and Kitty rubbed her hands on her face to see if she could get it off, before Mum saw her.

Now Kitty was a terrible sight, but still she said, 'I don't want to wash my face.'

'Do you like looking like a grub?' asked Mum.

'Yes, I do,' said Kitty. 'I want to be dirty. I like being dirty. I won't wash ever again!'

'Ugh, horrible!' said Dan. 'When you walk down the road everyone will run away.'

'Why?' asked Kitty.

'Because of the awful *smell*,' laughed Dan, and ran away when Kitty chased him round the table.

Mum put her head in her hands. At last she looked up and sighed. 'All right! You *stay* dirty!' She took Daniel upstairs to have his bath.

51

After a few minutes Kitty was bored in the kitchen. She crept upstairs, and listened outside the bathroom door. Daniel was making happy splashing noises, and Mum was talking to him quietly, and suddenly Kitty felt very sticky and uncomfortable. There were crumbs in her hair, and dirt on her arms, and earth on her T-shirt, and her legs itched where she had rolled in the grass. Kitty felt dirty. She was jealous of Dan for getting clean.

She hid round the corner when Mum took Daniel across the landing into his room—all wrapped cosily in the big white towel. Then Kitty slipped into the bathroom. The bath was still full of water, and Dan's best boat was floating in it, as well as two ducks. The boats and ducks looked clean. The bathwater was warm and inviting.

Kitty took off her shoes and socks, then stopped. Only her face, legs and arms were dirty, that was all. The rest of her was covered by the shorts and T-shirt, but *they* were covered with jam and earth.

Kitty had an idea. She would wash her clothes. So she jumped into the bath still wearing them, and lay down with the boat and ducks. Some of the water splashed over the side, but Kitty hoped it would clean the floor.

She grabbed the soap, but it didn't make enough foam. So she poured the whole of the bottle of shampoo down her front, and rubbed it into her clothes. That was better.

The flannel was on the washbasin, and Kitty couldn't reach it. So she pulled down the small white towel, dipped it in the bathwater, and used it to rub at her face, arms and legs. That was better, and anyway, it wasn't like a *real* wash.

Then Kitty looked at the dirty shoes and socks lying on the floor, and thought they needed a clean too. She climbed out of the bath, holding the wall so she would not slip, and threw the shoes and socks into the bath. The shoes floated. They were much better than Dan's silly old boat.

Just as Kitty was scrubbing at the muddy shoes with the smallest cleaning thing she could find—Dan's toothbrush—Mum came into the bathroom to pull out the plug. She seemed very surprised. All she could say was, 'Oh, Kitty. Oh, KITTY!'

Kitty pointed to her clean pink face. 'I did have my wash, Mum,' she said.

The Outlaws and the Triplets

Richmal Crompton

William's aunt's invitation was looked upon by William's family as little short of providential.

The Browns had decided not to go away that summer. They had decided that a holiday at home would be a pleasant change. The only drawback would be the presence of William. The presence of William was not compatible with that atmosphere of peace that is so necessary to a perfect holiday.

'Wouldn't it be *heavenly*,' said William's sister, Ethel, 'if someone would ask William somewhere for even a week? For next week specially.'

And she thought of the tennis party she had arranged to give the next week. She imagined the blissful feeling of security that William's absence would lend to it and compared it with her present feeling of gloomy certainty that everything was sure to go wrong. William, even when inspired by the best motives, seemed invariably to wreck every function which he attended, and he naturally expected to attend those held by his own family on their own premises. He was already deeply interested in the prospect of Ethel's tennis party.

'I'll think out some new sorts of games, Ethel,' he had volunteered, 'somethin' that'll make it go with a bit of a swing. I bet everyone's tired of tennis. I bet I can find somethin' more excitin' than that ole game.'

Ethel forbade him vehemently to meddle in her party. 'All I want you to do,' she told him sternly, 'is to keep out of the way.'

He said: 'All right,' meekly enough, but she had an uneasy suspicion that he was planning some surprise.

Mrs Brown, loyal to all her children even in the most trying circumstances, refused openly to admit the undesirability of William's presence.

'I'm sure that he'll be good, dear,' she said to Ethel. 'I'm certain he'll do his very best not to be a nuisance. But still,' she ended meditatively, 'it *would* be rather nice if Aunt Jane asked him to stay with her for a week or so. She's often said that she would.'

Great, therefore, was the jubilation in William's family when the invitation actually arrived. Then the jubilation died away. William refused to go. He said that he didn't want to miss Ethel's party. He was hurt and amazed by the general attitude.

'Well, *why* d'you want me to go?' he said. 'I should've thought this was just the time you *wouldn't* want me to go. I should've thought you'd all want me to stay and help with Ethel's party . . . *Me* upset things? '*Course* I won't upset things. I keep *tellin'* you I'm goin' to *help*. Well, I don't care what sort of a

good time Aunt Jane would give me, I don't want to miss Ethel's party. I don't *like* Aunt Jane, anyway. She kept askin' me history dates the last time I saw her. I'd much rather stay an' help Ethel with her party.'

He was adamant. It was impossible to send him away against his will. He didn't *want* to go to stay with Aunt Jane. He wanted to stay and help Ethel with her party.

His family spent hours of useless labour arguing with him. They pointed out the benefits that would accrue to him in the way of health and fresh interests from the change. He refused to be moved from his position. He didn't want to go to stay with Aunt Jane (he repeated *ad nauseam* that she had asked him history dates the last time he had seen her) and he did want to stay and help Ethel with her party.

In the end his family, worn out by argument, surrendered, and Mrs Brown wrote to Aunt Jane a letter of such consummate tact that Aunt Jane replied saying that she thought it just a little selfish of dear Ethel to insist on William's staying at home so that he could help her with the preparations for her party, but that she would expect dear William as soon as Ethel could manage without him, and all they would have to do would be to send a wire, and would Mrs Brown give dear

William her love and tell him that she would have known how much he longed to see her even without his dear mother's telling her.

Gloomily, therefore, Ethel surrendered to Fate. William was amused by her attitude.

'Wait till the time comes,' he said, 'you'll be *jolly* glad I didn't go away. There'll never have *been* such a party.'

This ominous prophecy did not lessen Ethel's foreboding, and her dejection increased as the day of the party approached. She watched William with morbid interest.

'Are there any infectious diseases he hasn't had, mother?' she asked, a far-away hope springing up in her breast.

'Not many,' said his mother, and understanding the trend of Ethel's question, added: 'If he got anything, you know, dear, we'd all have to be in quarantine.'

The faint, far-away hope died down in Ethel's breast.

It so happened that William had formed no actual plans for enlivening the party. He merely considered it his duty to get a little more 'go' into it than there had been in her last one—a very dull affair, he considered, in which the guests had merely played tennis or sat about and talked.

He was on his way to meet his Outlaws now, and he meant to discuss

the situation with them fully. They were waiting for him in the road outside Henry's house—all but Henry, whose voice was heard within the garden raised in passionate altercation with his mother.

'Well, why must I? Why can't someone else take it out?'

'I keep *telling* you, dear. There's no one else to take her out. Nannie's gone to bed with a headache, and I can't leave the house.'

'Why can't she stay in the garden?' said Henry.

'She's been in the garden all morning and she's tired of it. She won't be any trouble. You ought to *like* taking out your little sister in her pram, Henry. You ought to be *proud* of her.'

'Well, I'm jolly well not,' retorted Henry. 'I'm *sick* of her—pulling my hair and taking all my things and getting me into rows by yelling if ever I try to do anything back.'

'*Henry!*' The voice was deeply shocked. 'How *can* you talk like that! There never was such a sweet baby. Hundreds of little boys would give anything to have her for a sister.'

'I wish they could have her then, that's all,' said Henry bitterly. 'Oh, all right, I'll take her.'

'That's a good boy. Keep her out about half an hour. And remember to call at the grocer's for the tea.'

Walking slowly and gloomily, Henry came down the garden path, pushing a pram.

His three friends surveyed him without enthusiasm.

'She made me bring it,' he said. 'An' I've got to go to the grocer's. Well, you needn't come with me if you don't want.'

But the Outlaws, though acutely sensible of the ignominy of the proceeding, did not intend to forsake him.

'Oh, we'll come all right,' said William, 'but anyone with a bit of *sense* would have got out of it somehow. Why din't you say you'd hurt your wrist?'

''Cause she knows I haven't,' answered Henry simply.

'Well, why din't you say you felt too ill?'

''Cause I'd rather come out an' push a pram than go to bed. An' I've told you you needn't come if you don't want to.'

They walked along the road in a somewhat gloomy silence. It was difficult to sustain their usual characters of brigands or pirates in the face of Henry's pram.

It was William's idea to pretend that it was a gun-carriage and that they were hastening with it to the relief of a beleaguered army. They pushed it in turns and ran with it at a quick trot.

Its occupant seemed to find the movement soporific and was fast asleep by the time they reached the grocer's. Ginger had had twopence given him by his mother for rolling the lawn, and they all went into the grocer's to help him choose some sweets. Henry bought the tea and put it for safety into his pocket, then they chose some boiled sweets of a particularly cheap and colourful brand. They next held a spirited exchange of grimaces with the grocer's boy, which degenerated into a scuffle and brought down a pyramid of tins of boot blacking. The grocer chased them out of the shop, and they emerged into the road feeling cheered and exhilarated.

It was Ginger's turn to push the pram, and he seized it with a new vigour.

'She'll yell if she wakes,' Henry warned him, so Ginger abated his vigour somewhat.

'Look here,' said William, 'I've not thought of anything exciting to do at Ethel's party tomorrow yet. Let's all try an' think of somethin'.'

'Let's all dress up as robbers an' dash in at them,' suggested Ginger.

'Let's set some mice loose among them,' said Henry, 'I can get some mice.'

'Let's put a grass snake on the tea-table,' said Douglas. 'That'd scare 'em stiff.'

'But I want something they'd *enjoy*,' said William.

'Well, they'd enjoy all those things,' said Ginger, 'they'd enjoy talking about them an' tellin' other people about them afterwards, even if they didn't enjoy them at the time. It'd be somethin' to make them remember the party by; if a party's ordinary and dull, there's nothin' to make people *remember* it by.'

'An' I'll tell you another thing,' said Douglas. 'And that's letting a bit of gunpowder off while they're having tea. That's *great* fun for them. And another is putting glue on the hats, so that when they go home they can't get their hats off. I bet they'd laugh like anything at that —'

They had reached Henry's house now, and Henry, stopping short, began to gaze with startled interest at the sleeping baby.

'I say!' he cried excitedly.

He craned further into the pram. When he withdrew his face was pale with horror.

'I say,' he said, 'that's not ours.'

'Not your what?' said William.

'Not our baby,' said Henry.

''*Course* it is,' said William, 'what makes you think it isn't?'

'Ours doesn't look like that.'

'There isn't any difference in babies,' said William, 'they all look just the same. You can't *possibly* tell any diff'rence.'

'I can,' protested Henry vehemently. 'When you know them *very* well there is a difference, and I tell you, this one isn't ours.'

'Well, I bet your mother won't know,' said William. 'I bet *she* won't see any difference. It looks just the same to me, an' I bet it looks just the same to anyone.'

'I tell you it *doesn't*,' said Henry, 'and its clothes are different. She'll see its clothes are different anyway.'

William realized the force of this argument.

'Couldn't we say we'd bought it some new clothes for a present?' he suggested, not very convincingly.

'No,' said Henry rather irritably. 'She'd know we couldn't have. An' I keep tellin' you she knows its face.'

'Well, I believe it's the same one,' said William. 'You've just got muddled, that's all it is. You're trying to swank, pretending that you can tell a difference in babies when everyone knows there isn't any. How *could* it be a different one anyway? We just took it to the shop and brought it back. How could it have got changed?'

'It isn't our pram either,' said Henry, who was closely examining the equipage, 'it's quite different.'

'There *was* another pram outside the shop,' said Ginger, thoughtfully, 'p'raps I took the wrong one.'

'I'll run back and see if ours is there,' said Henry.

He ran off down the road and soon reappeared, paler than ever.

'There isn't any pram at all there now,' he said. 'I've been right in the shop and there's *nothing*.' He glanced with distaste at the infant who still slept peacefully in the pram. 'Well, I can't take *that* one home. She'd kick up an *awful* row.'

'Look here,' said William, 'I expect someone took yours by mistake. I expect it's always happening. Well, they *do* all look just the same whatever you say—so of *course* it's always happening. I expect no one ever ends up a single day with the same baby they started out with . . . an' I don't see what you're making all this fuss about. It's a *baby*, isn't it? Well, what more d'you want? What does it matter if it's not the same as the other? Someone else has got the other, so *they're* all right, an' *you're* all right. Oh, very well . . . if you say your mother'd make a fuss . . . Well, I'll go round the village an' try'n' find yours.'

'An' I'll go round the other way,' said Ginger.

They set off with a purposeful air in opposite directions.

Henry and Douglas were left with the pram and the sleeping stranger. Henry kept throwing uneasy glances through the hedge.

'I say,' he said, 'I'm scared stiff she'll come out after the tea and see it's the wrong one. She'll go *mad*. You don't know what they're like about babies. Put it here where the hedge is nice and thick an' I'll go in and give her the tea and tell her that we're taking the baby out for a bit of a walk. She'll be jolly glad because she's busy, and it's generally out till tea-time.'

Cautiously he entered the gate. Soon the voice of his mother was wafted through the hedge to the waiting Douglas.

'How *could* you be so careless, Henry! I simply daren't *think* of what might have happened . . . Just going off like that and forgetting all about her! I shall never, never, *never* trust you with her again. Yes, Mrs Hanshaw brought her back a minute ago. Found her outside the grocer's shop. Fortunately she's still asleep. You simply aren't fit to be trusted with *anything*.'

Henry rejoined Douglas in the road,

and they stood gazing at each other in helpless dismay. At that moment there reappeared the figure of William jauntily wheeling another pram.

'I say,' he called exultantly, 'I bet this is it. I found it outside another shop.'

At the same moment there appeared from the other direction the figure of Ginger. He, too, was wheeling a pram.

He did not at first see William. He called out:

'It's all right. I've got it. I found it outside a house.'

Henry looked from one to the other, a nightmarish grin on his face.

'Which is yours?' said William. 'I bet mine is.'

'I bet *mine* is,' put in Ginger.

'Neither is,' said Henry, 'we've got ours. Someone brought it back.'

They gazed at the three prams with their sleeping cargoes, and the situation in all its horror gradually dawned upon them.

'Gosh!' said William. '*Three!*'

'We'd better take 'em back,' said Ginger faintly.

'My mother was *mad* about ours,' said Henry.

There came to William and Ginger a vision of three raging mothers.

'We can't take 'em back,' said William apprehensively. 'I vote—I vote we take them to the police station and say that we found someone kidnapping 'em and rescued 'em.'

'They won't believe us,' said Ginger sadly.

William on reflection agreed that probably they wouldn't.

'What are we going to *do* then?' demanded Douglas.

At that moment the voice of Henry's mother was heard urgently calling him.

'I'd better go,' said Henry, 'she'll only be coming out after me if I don't, and then she'll find all these others and kick up another row.'

They agreed, and, with something of relief at his heart, Henry left the pram-infested scene. Douglas, Ginger, and William were left each with his attendant infant. They looked at each other helplessly.

'I vote we just leave them here an' creep away,' said Ginger.

'We can't leave them outside Henry's house,' said William. 'It'd only get him into another row. Let's take them down the road a bit and leave them there.'

Despondently they began to wheel their prams down the road.

'I bet wherever we leave them we'll get into a row,' said William gloomily. 'Someone'll be sure to see us with them. Seems 'str'ordin'ry to me that some people seem to have nothin' else to do but watch other people doin' things an' then tell about them afterwards to get 'em into rows.'

At that moment a boy came alongside of them pushing a pram in a detached and hasty manner.

'Hello,' he said, 'you got to take *yours* to the baby show, too?'

William made a non-committal sound.

'Well, I think it's the limit, don't you?' said the boy. 'I said why should I take it, and she said that she'd entered it and so it had to go, but she'd got a bad headache an' couldn't take it, and that I ought to be *proud* to take my little brother to a baby show an' a lot of stuff like that. Said it was sure to get a prize. Yes, it'll get a prize for yelling all right if it starts. Well, I don't want to be longer than I can help making a fool of myself pushing a beastly pram so I'll get on.'

He continued his hurried and detached progress. He walked quickly and airily by the side of the pram, keeping two fingers only upon the handle to steer it and determinedly looking in the opposite direction, as if

hoping to convince those he met that he had no connection whatever with the equipage and that it merely happened to be going of its own volition in the same direction. Somewhat cheered by this spectacle, William, Ginger, and Douglas began to follow after him in a row, each pushing his pram.

'A baby show,' said William, 'that'll be fine. We can just put them with the other prams an' leave them there. You see with a lot of prams, no one'll notice three extra ones. We can just put 'em there an' creep away.'

The boy in front with a deft and practised movement of his wrist had turned his pram into the gateway of a large garden. There on the lawn was a serried row of prams. The Outlaws put theirs at the end as unobtrusively as possible. No one seemed to have noticed their arrival. Several groups of women were standing about on the lawn talking.

'Now let's go,' whispered William. 'We'd better not all go at once or they'll see. We'll go one by one . . . You go now, Ginger.'

Ginger crept away in his best Red Indian style.

No one noticed his departure.

'Now you, Douglas,' hissed William.

Douglas crept away with equal success. William watched his figure as it

slunk through the bushes and then out through the gateway. He leant negligently on his pram handles waiting till Douglas should be quite out of sight. Then, just as he had decided to follow, he heard himself addressed in a sharp, imperious voice.

'Are you in charge of these prams?' An elegant woman in a long, black satin cloak and be-plumed hat stood in front of him, pointing a pair of lorgnettes at him.

The proprietary attitude in which William was leaning over his pram handles made the charge a difficult one to deny.

'Er—yes,' he said guardedly, 'I mean, I'm sort of in charge of them.'

'Why aren't there any numbers on them then?'

'I don't know,' said William.

The woman turned to another harassed-looking woman behind her.

'The whole thing's been most disgracefully mismanaged. Here are three more prams without numbers. I said particularly: "Send the numbers round to the mothers beforehand so as to save time." Were no numbers sent?' she said to William.

'No,' said William.

A third woman came up and meekly affixed numbers to the prams.

The first woman was looking at William rather doubtfully.

'Did you say you were in charge of all three prams?' she said.

'Yes,' replied William.

'I suppose one of them is your little brother?' she went on.

'They all are,' said William, who thought that, cornered as he was, he might as well accept the situation in its entirety. It was never William's way to go in for half measures.

The lady looked at them still more doubtfully.

'Triplets?' she said.

William again made his non-committal noise. The lady evidently took it to mean assent.

'How curious to have them in three separate prams! You couldn't have brought them *all* surely?'

'Yes, I did,' said William. 'I push one pram for a bit along the road and then I fetch the second up to it, and then I fetch the third. And then I start again on the first.'

'How very strange!' said the woman. 'I should have thought it would be

simpler to put them all in one large pram. They're quite small children. Why didn't your mother come with them?'

'She's ill,' said William.

'I'm so sorry. I'm sure you're a great help to her with your three little brothers, aren't you?'

'Oh, yes,' said William, now firmly established in his own mind as brother to the three sleeping infants.

'Well, do suggest to her that she puts them all in one large pram. It wouldn't be a bit overcrowded. And really taking out three prams in the way you describe seems an unnecessary labour—till they've got *much* older than this, anyway. Have you brought the form?'

'The form?' said William.

'Yes. Surely a form was sent to your mother for her to fill in?'

'No, it wasn't,' said William.

'*There!*' said the woman again. 'Another muddle. The thing's been *completely* mismanaged. Give me a form, please.' The meek woman handed her a form. 'And I ought to have been told that there would be triplets. They're a class by themselves, of course. I'll fill in the form now. Just answer the questions,' she said to William, 'and I'll fill in the answers. What illnesses have they had?'

'Lumbago,' said William, remem-

bering the complaint that had kept his father in bed for a day last week.

'*What?*'

'No, not lumbago,' said William hastily. 'I mean only one of them had lumbago just a bit. No, the illness that the other two had is —' he paused a moment. What was that thing that had kept Colonel Fortescue in bed all last holidays, and so left the Outlaws in unofficial possession of his paddock? 'Oh, I know, gout.'

'Rubbish,' said the woman indignantly. 'Children of that age couldn't have gout.'

'The doctor said he'd never known one have it before,' argued William.

At the mention of the doctor the woman became less sure of her ground.

'Well, all I can say is *I've* never heard of it,' she said and passed on hastily to the next question. 'What have they been brought up on?'

'Brought up on?' said William.

'Yes, what do they eat?'

'Oh,' said William, comprehending, 'well, for breakfast they have sausages.'

'*Sausages!*' said the lady horrified.

William realized that sausages was wrong.

'Only one of them has sausages,' he said reassuringly, 'the others have chops.'

'*Chops!*'

Evidently chops was wrong, too.

'I only meant one of the other two has chops,' said William, hastily, 'this one has kippers.'

'*Kippers!*'

Evidently kippers was wrong, too. But at that moment one of the triplets awoke with a yell, and at once the other two, roused from sleep, joined in the chorus. Also at that minute William, turning sharply, saw three angry-looking women entering the gate. They were obviously mothers on the track of their missing young. Without a second's hesitation William dived into the bushes, plunged through the hedge, scrambled out into the road, and ran as fast as he could in the direction of his home. He had no doubt at all that the mothers would discover who he was and where he lived and all about him, but it would take a little time.

'Mother,' he said breathlessly, entering the drawing-room, 'I'll go and stay with Aunt Jane if I can go at once.'

'Whatever's made you change your mind, dear?'

William tried to compose his features into their expression of shining virtue.

'Because you said you'd like me to go, and I want to please you.'

Mrs Brown looked slightly bewildered.

'Well, dear, I'll write to her tonight, and you can go to her tomorrow.'

'No,' said William, 'I want to go there now, at once, this minute. It won't be any use tomorrow.'

Mrs Brown looked still more bewildered.

'But why, dear?' she said.

'Because,' said William unctuously, 'I may not feel like this tomorrow. I just feel now that I want to please you and do what you want me to do, but I don't know how long a feeling like that's going to last. It doesn't last very long generally. I'm beginning to feel it going already. If I don't get off to Aunt Jane's now this minute, it'll have gone.'

Mrs Brown's thoughts went to Ethel. Ethel would find it very difficult to forgive her if she let slip this chance, appearing so miraculously and at the last minute, of a Williamless tennis party . . .

'Very well, dear,' she said, 'I'll go and pack your things this minute. We'll send the wire from the station.'

William was standing by the window, keeping an anxious eye on the point in the road where the three angry mothers would appear.

'Do be quick,' he said, 'I can feel that feeling going already . . .'

In an incredibly short space of time Mrs Brown was downstairs with his bag.

'Come along, dear,' she said, 'you needn't bother to change. We can just get the bus into Hadley and catch the four o'clock train.'

They hurried to the end of the road and just caught the bus. As they sat there waiting for it to start, three angry-looking women wheeling prams were seen to turn into the lane that led to William's home. Mrs Brown watched them with interest.

'I wonder where they're going,' she said, then, 'why, they're going to our house. How funny . . . Yes, they're going up to our front door. I wonder what they want.'

But William was gazing dreamily in front of him as if he did not hear her, and at that moment the bus started.

They just had time to wire to William's aunt before catching the train. William waved to his mother till the train took him out of her sight, then sank back into his corner of the carriage with a sigh of relief. His mother would be on her way home where the three angry women awaited her . . . They couldn't do anything to him now, of course, and they'd probably have forgotten all about it by the time he came home. It was a pity about Ethel's party. It would just have to be the dull sort of affair it usually was. Aunt Jane's . . . she was jolly dull, of course, but still he might manage to have quite a decent time. There was a pond in her garden, in which he could be ship-wrecked from a raft, and a rockery that might be made to represent an impregnable mountain lair. There was a fat Pekinese in the opposite house into whose ordered life considerable excitement might be introduced.

William began to look forward with feelings of pleasurable anticipation to his visit to Aunt Jane.

The Kidnapping of Clarissa Montgomery

ROBIN KLEIN

'You'll only have to stay here till your rich guardian pays the ransom,' said the kidnapper, whose name was Humphrey. He felt rather sorry for poor little Clarissa. She hadn't said anything since they'd grabbed her from the luxurious grounds of her mansion that afternoon. 'I think the poor little kid's in shock,' Humphrey said worriedly to Spud, who had masterminded the abduction. Spud didn't care if she was in shock, neither did Milligan.

'Just sit tight and don't cause any trouble, kid,' Spud snarled. 'Soon as the old man pays the fifty thousand, you'll be sent back.'

Clarissa finally spoke. 'Fifty thousand?' she said.

'I'm sure he'll manage to find it,' said kind-hearted Humphrey reassuringly. 'You'll be out of here in no time.'

Clarissa looked at him coldly. 'You're all mad,' she said. 'You could have got a whole lot more than fifty thousand. My guardian is loaded.'

She's in shock, Humphrey thought, and made her a cup of cocoa with his own hands. He'd fixed up a corner of the barn quite nicely with a toffee apple in a saucer. He was fond of little kids.

Spud was setting up a poker game. Clarissa watched silently.

'You don't have to be scared of those gorillas,' Humphrey whispered. 'They're really harmless.'

'I'm not scared of anything,' Clarissa said, and drew closer to the table.

'Beat it,' growled Spud, but Clarissa looked at his cards, then went

round the table and inspected Humphrey's and Milligan's. 'Get rid of the red queen and keep the clubs,' she said to Humphrey, and he did, and won.

'Scat, kid,' said Spud, but Clarissa sat down at the table.

'I want to play, too,' she said.

'Go back to your cocoa,' Spud ordered, but Clarissa opened her mouth and let out a high-pitched wailing yell. It went on and on, unbearable in the galvanized-iron roofed barn, and Spud, Milligan, and Humphrey covered their ears.

'Maybe she'll stop if we let her play,' suggested Humphrey, and dealt out a hand to Clarissa. She stopped screeching and picked up her cards. Then she proceeded, without any trouble at all, to win ten games and fifty dollars.

'It's not very nice, if you ask me,' Spud said disgustedly. 'Little girls shouldn't know how to cheat at poker.'

Clarissa pocketed her winnings and went to bed. She slept very well. In the morning she woke up early. Humphrey, Spud, and Milligan were dozing fitfully in uncomfortable chairs. Clarissa made herself a substantial breakfast, then examined the barn.

'Get away from that door!' Spud said, waking up.

'I've seen play forts in council parks better defended than this old barn,' Clarissa scoffed. 'The police could have this place surrounded and you wouldn't even know. No wonder you only asked for fifty thousand. It's all you're worth.'

Spud was so indignant that he bit his pre-breakfast cigar in two. 'What became of all the food?' he demanded angrily.

'I had it for my breakfast, of course,' Clarissa said.

So Humphrey, Spud, and Milligan had to make do with discussing the plans for collecting the ransom money instead. Clarissa listened. 'It won't work,' she jeered. 'Just how do you expect Humphrey to reach the hollow tree in the park past a whole lot of detectives all lying in wait? It's too corny, collecting ransom money from a hollow tree.'

'And what would you suggest then, Miss Smarty?' Spud asked.

'Some place where they can't set up an ambush, of course. Tell them to put the money in a briefcase in a plastic bag and drop it off the pier. One of you could get it wearing scuba gear. It's a much better plan than your old hollow tree. I'll draft a new anonymous letter to my rich guardian.' Clarissa began cutting letters from Spud's newspaper, even though he hadn't read the racing page yet. She pasted the letters to a sheet of paper, and even Spud had to admit that it looked much more professional than theirs. And she'd doubled the ransom money, too.

'But none of us can scuba dive,' Humphrey pointed out.

'I can,' said Clarissa crushingly. 'I'll collect the money. But only if you give me a share.'

'That's only right,' said Humphrey. 'If she picks it up, she should be given something.'

'Ninety-five per cent,' said Clarissa. 'Or I won't go at all. Anyhow, you wouldn't have any ransom money in the first place, if it wasn't for me.'

'If it wasn't for you, we wouldn't be sitting in this draughty old barn with nothing to eat for breakfast but a toffee apple,' said Spud. 'I wish we'd concentrated on stealing your rich guardian's valuable oil paintings instead.'

'You'd never get near them. They're fitted with electronic alarms.'

'I stole the Mona Lisa once,' Spud said boastfully.

'And you only got as far as the front door before they caught you. I read about it in the papers. The only way you could steal my guardian's paintings is if I came along and showed you the secret panel where you can cut off the alarm circuit. So there.'

Spud sourly began a round of poker while Humphrey went out to deliver the ransom note. Clarissa won another ten games. Spud thought with pleasure that after tonight they'd be rid of her. 'Soon as we pick up that briefcase, we'll drop you off at your mansion,' he said.

'First we'll come back here and count the money,' contradicted Clarissa. 'Don't you know you can't trust anyone? You're the most hopeless gang leader I ever met. And you'll have to make plans about leaving the country, too. You'll need to learn a foreign language, but that's no problem. This afternoon you can all study French verbs. I'll supervise. That's after you clean up the getaway car. I'm not going anywhere to pick up ransom money in a car as dirty as that.'

She nagged so much that Spud, Humphrey, and Milligan went out in the cold and cleaned the car. Clarissa sat at the window and made sure they did a thorough job. Spud, Milligan, and Humphrey consoled themselves with thinking of all the goodies they'd buy once they got their hands on the ransom money. 'A farm in France,' Spud said. 'I always wanted one of those.'

'I bet you don't know anything about farming, or France,' said Clarissa. 'It might be a good idea if I came along to advise you. I always give my guardian advice on real estate and money investment and I practically run his affairs for him. I don't know what he'd do without me.'

Milligan, Spud, and even Humphrey eyed her with distaste. They were getting fed up with the draughty barn, the waiting and the French verbs, and most of all they were fed up with Clarissa and her organizing.

It was almost a relief when the time came to collect the ransom money. They drove to the waterfront, and Clarissa put on the scuba suit and galloped confidently into the sea.

'She might swim to the pier and just pop up and give the alarm,' said Humphrey nervously. 'Let's get out of here.'

'Not without our share of the money,' said Spud. 'I haven't put up with that kid all day for nothing.'

'We won't have to put up with her much longer,' said Milligan thankfully. 'Soon as we sort out the ransom money, we can drop her off at her mansion, and good riddance. Then it's off to the south of France for us.'

'That guardian's welcome to her,' said Spud. 'We should give the poor old fellow a few thousand dollars back. I feel sorry for him, having to put up with her till she's grown up and married.'

'No one would marry her,' said Milligan with conviction. 'Not even if they were bribed with all of the Montgomery fortune.'

They watched the water anxiously, but no police boat bristling with armed constables skimmed into sight. And after fifteen minutes, Clarissa emerged, carrying a weighted briefcase in a plastic bag. Milligan, Spud,

and Humphrey tried to grab it from her, but Clarissa put it in the getaway car and sat on it. 'Don't be so greedy,' she said. 'You're making as much noise as kids in a sandpit. You'll just have to wait till we get back to the barn.'

On the way back the three gangsters were quite civil to Clarissa. They were all thinking that very soon they could drop her off at her mansion and never have to listen to her again or be ordered about.

Spud had the first try at the locked briefcase, and failed. Milligan failed, too, and then Humphrey had a turn, with his skilful hands that had foiled every bank safe in town. But even he couldn't get the combination lock open.

'What a lot of butterfingers!' said Clarissa, and turned the little numbered cylinder and the lid flew open.

But the briefcase wasn't full of bank notes at all. There wasn't anything but the bricks that had served to weigh it down in the water. And one short typed note. Spud snatched it up and read it aloud, and his eyes rounded with horror and disbelief.

DO NOT WANT CLARISSA BACK, SHE IS TOO

IRRITATING AND BOSSY. YOU CAN KEEP HER.

GLAD TO GET RID OF HER,

REGARDS, ALGERNON MONTGOMERY, MILLIONAIRE

All the kidnappers turned pale and sat down.

'Why are you all sitting down wasting time?' Clarissa demanded, frowning. 'We have an oil painting job to plan. And now that I'm in charge of this gang, I expect much better work from all of you.'

Mighty Mountain and the Three Strong Women

IRENE HEDLUND

English version by Judith Elkin

Many years ago in a small village in Japan, a huge baby was born. He was so big that everyone called him Baby Mountain.

By the time he was twelve, he was the biggest, strongest boy in the school and the wrestling champion of the whole village. The people in the village were proud of their enormous champion and called him Mighty Mountain.

One warm autumn day, Mighty Mountain decided he must leave the village. He would go to the capital and become a famous wrestler. Every year, the Emperor held a grand wrestling match to find the strongest man in all Japan. Mighty Mountain was sure that he could win.

It was a long walk to the capital and Mighty Mountain strode along, humming to himself. At each step, the ground shook, birds fell from the trees, and animals scurried away in terror.

Mighty Mountain didn't even notice. He was too busy thinking how wonderful he was. Everyone loved him because he was so big and strong. He was quite sure that he was the best-looking wrestler in all Japan, but of course he was far too modest to boast about it.

Just then, Mighty Mountain noticed a girl filling her bucket with water. She was very pretty, with pink cheeks, shining black hair and sparkling eyes.

As the girl climbed on to the footpath in front of him, Mighty Mountain grinned to himself. What fun it would be to tickle her and make her spill the water. Perhaps he could walk home with her and help her to carry the bucket.

Mighty Mountain crept up behind the girl and poked a giant finger in her side. The girl squealed and giggled, but

she didn't spill the water. Then, before
Mighty Mountain could move away,
she trapped his massive hand under her
arm.

Mighty Mountain was delighted.
Playful as well as pretty, he thought. He
tried to pull his hand away, but it
wouldn't budge. He pulled harder.

'Let me go,' he laughed. 'You're very
strong for a girl, but I don't want to
hurt you.'

'Oh, don't worry about that,' giggled
the girl, 'I love strong men. Try pulling
harder.' She smiled sweetly at him.

But the harder he pulled and tugged,
the tighter the girl's grip seemed to get.
She began to walk on, dragging the
wrestler behind her.

'Please, let me go,' he begged. 'I'm
Mighty Mountain, strongest and
bravest of all the wrestlers and I'm on
my way to take part in the Emperor's
Wrestling Match.'

'Oh, you must come and meet
Grandma, then. You seem tired. Let
me carry you to our house.'

'Certainly not. Just let me go!'

The girl stopped and seemed to look
right inside him.

'I'm sure you're a good wrestler,' she
said kindly, 'but what will you do when
you meet someone who is really
strong? You've got three months before
the wrestling match. I know because
Grandma thought of taking part. If you

come home with me now, we could make you into the strongest man in all Japan. Otherwise, you will only spend all your time in bad company and lose what little strength you've got.'

'I don't need help from you, or Grandma, or anyone else,' roared Mighty Mountain, but a tiny shadow of doubt had begun to creep into his mind. He *was* feeling tired and his knees had gone quite weak. If he refused to go with the girl, she might easily break his arm or throw him down the steep mountainside.

He nodded wearily. The girl let him go. He peered down miserably at his red, swollen hand and wondered what he had let himself in for.

They came at last to a small thatched hut high up in the mountains. The girl pointed to two tiny feet in the doorway. Grandma was having her afternoon nap.

Round the corner of the hut came a woman carrying a cow on one shoulder. It was the girl's mother, back from working in the fields. When she caught sight of them, she put the cow down and hurriedly brushed the cowhair off her clothes.

'The poor cow gets sore feet, if I let her walk on the stony paths,' she explained to the astonished Mighty Mountain. 'Who is this nice young man, Kuniko?'

Kuniko told her. The two women walked around the wrestler, looking him up and down. Mighty Mountain giggled nervously and puffed out his chest and arms to show his huge muscles.

'Mm,' said Mother, 'he looks delicate. He needs some proper food.'

Then Kuniko called Grandma. She shouted very loudly because Grandma was a little deaf. The tiny feet started to kick furiously.

'All right, all right, I'm coming!'

A tiny, very wrinkled, toothless old lady shuffled out, leaning heavily on a stick. She stumbled over the roots of the great oak tree in the yard.

'Ow . . . ow . . . ow . . .' she muttered. 'My eyes aren't what they used to be. That's the third time this week I've bumped into that silly old tree.'

She put her thin arms round the trunk and pulled it straight out of the ground.

'Throw it away, dear,' she said to her daughter, 'I don't think my poor old back could manage it. Mind it doesn't get in anyone's way. You know how clumsy you are.'

Kuniko's mother threw the tree. It flew through the air like a rocket, getting smaller and smaller until it landed on the far mountainside.

Mighty Mountain could stand no

more. His face went pale, his eyes glazed over and his massive legs trembled. Suddenly, with a terrific thump, he crumpled to the ground.

Mighty Mountain had fainted.

Grandma noticed him for the first time, as he crashed at her feet. 'Who's this?' she cackled.

Kuniko gently cradled Mighty Mountain in her arms. 'Poor weak man,' she whispered. 'Do you think we could get him ready for the ring in only three months?'

Grandma sighed. 'Well, it's not long,' she said, 'and he's a feeble-looking fellow.' She bent down and flung him over her shoulder. Leaning heavily on her stick, she hobbled back into the hut and threw him on the bed.

The next day, the three women set to work.

Very early every morning, Kuniko dragged Mighty Mountain out of bed and made him bathe in the icy stream. Each day, Mother boiled his rice in less and less water, until he could eat food no ordinary man could even chew. Grandma made him work harder and harder and carry heavier and heavier loads.

Every evening, Mighty Mountain practised wrestling with Grandma. Grandma was so old and frail that she couldn't do him too much harm. The exercise might even help her rheumatism.

As the days grew colder and colder and autumn turned to winter, Mighty Mountain got stronger and stronger, almost without noticing. Soon he could pull up trees almost as easily as Grandma could. He could even throw them, but not very far.

Before wrestling practice, Mighty Mountain stamped his foot on the ground. Then the villagers down below looked up at the winter sky and wondered why the thunder was rumbling round the mountains so late in the year.

One evening, Mighty Mountain managed to hold Grandma down on the ground for half a minute.

Grandma's face broke into a thousand wrinkles as she cackled loudly. Kuniko shrieked with excitement and hugged him, almost breaking his ribs. Mother slapped him on the back, making his eyes water.

They all agreed that Mighty Mountain was ready to take part in the Emperor's Wrestling Match.

'We want you to take the cow,' said Mother. 'Sell her and buy yourself a belt of silk, the thickest and heaviest you can find. If you wear it when you greet the Emperor, it will remind you of us and bring you luck.'

Mighty Mountain looked worried. 'I can't take the cow. How will you plough the fields?'

Grandma almost fell over laughing. Kuniko giggled, 'We don't use the cow for work. Mother is five times stronger than any cow. We only keep the cow because she's got such beautiful brown eyes.'

'She's very pretty,' agreed Mother, 'but it's hard work carrying her down to the valley every day to find grass.'

'Then if I earn any money at the Wrestling Match, you shall have it.'

Kuniko blushed, 'Oh, no,' she said, 'we can't take money from a stranger.'

Mighty Mountain grinned at her, bowed low to Grandma and asked if he could marry Kuniko and become one of the family.

Kuniko clapped her hands with joy. Grandma and Mother pretended to give the matter deep and serious consideration, then, with big smiles, they agreed.

'We'll even let you beat us at wrestling sometimes.'

The very next morning, Mighty Mountain tied his hair in a fancy topknot, thanked Mother, threw Grandma up in the air just for fun, and playfully tickled Kuniko.

He ran off down the mountain carrying the cow and waving until he could no longer see the three women.

At the first town he came to, Mighty Mountain sold the cow. She had never worked, so she was good and fat, and fetched a high price. With the money, he bought the thickest and heaviest silk belt he could find. Then he headed towards the capital.

Mighty Mountain hardly noticed the cold as he crunched through the snow in his bare feet. He was too busy thinking of Kuniko and Mother and Grandma.

When he reached the Emperor's Palace, he found that the other wrestlers were already there. They were lazing about, preening themselves, eating large bowls of soft rice, telling fantastic stories and comparing their enormous weights and their huge stomachs. No one took any notice of Mighty Mountain.

In the Palace Yard, the ladies-in-waiting and courtiers waited for the wrestling to begin. They wore layers and layers of clothes, so heavy with gold and embroidery that they could hardly move. The ladies-in-waiting wore thick white make-up, and the false eyebrows painted high on their foreheads made them look surprised all the time.

The Emperor sat as still as a statue and all alone behind a screen. He was far too aloof and dignified to be seen by ordinary people. The wrestling bored him. He much preferred reading and writing poetry and hoped the wrestling would soon be over.

The first match was between Mighty Mountain and Balloon Belly, a wrestler who was famous for his gigantic stomach.

With great ceremony, the two wrestlers threw a little salt into the ring to drive away evil spirits. Then they stood, legs apart, facing each other.

Balloon Belly rippled his enormous stomach then raised his foot and stamped the ground with a terrific crash. He glared at Mighty Mountain, as if to say, 'Beat that, weakling!'

Mighty Mountain glared back at Balloon Belly, thought of Grandma and stamped his foot. It sounded like a clap of thunder. The ground shook and Balloon Belly floated out of the ring like a giant green soap bubble. He landed with a thud in front of the Emperor's screen.

'The Earth God is angry,' Balloon Belly stammered, bowing low to the screen, 'I think there's something wrong with the salt. I had better not wrestle again this year.'

Five other wrestlers thought the Earth God might be angry with them, too, and decided not to wrestle.

When the next competitor was ready, Mighty Mountain was careful not to stamp his foot too hard. He just picked his opponent up round the waist and carried him out of the ring.

With a polite bow, Mighty Mountain placed the wrestler in front of the Emperor's screen. Then, one by one, he did exactly the same with all the other wrestlers.

The ladies-in-waiting looked more surprised than ever as they giggled delightedly behind their fans.

The Emperor's shoulders heaved with silent laughter and the plume on his head-dress wobbled in a most undignified manner. He hadn't seen anything so funny for years. He put one royal finger through the screen and waggled it at the wrestlers who were sitting on the ground blubbering. He gave orders for Mighty Mountain to receive all the prize money.

The Emperor congratulated Mighty Mountain. 'But,' he whispered, 'I don't think you had better take part again next year. We don't want to upset these poor babies any more.' He looked at the heap of wrestlers and started giggling again.

Mighty Mountain agreed quite happily. He had decided that he would much rather be a farmer anyway, and he hurried off back to Kuniko.

Kuniko saw him coming from a long way off and ran to meet him. She hugged him carefully, then picked him up and carried him and the heavy bag of money half-way up the mountain. Then she put him down and let him carry her the rest of the way home.

The name of Mighty Mountain was soon forgotten in the capital. But the Emperor never really enjoyed another wrestling match and was always glad when it was over and he could get back to his poetry.

Now and again, the people in the village down below feel the earth shake and hear thunder rumbling round the mountains. But it's only Mighty Mountain and Grandma practising their wrestling.

'I didn't, Miss.'

'Anne, do be quiet! And stop bleeding all over the place.'

'Yes, Miss.'

'Claire, let me ask you something. Would you mind standing on this chair now and showing me what Kevin Jackson taught Anne?'

'No, Miss. I mean, yes, Miss. I don't want to.'

'I'm sure you don't! And why don't you?'

'It looks funny, Miss.'

'I see. Well, if that's all that's bothering you, you can face the other way.'

'It hurts, Miss.'

'Then bite it gently. Just climb on the chair, face the other way, and bite your nose *gently*. And tell me when you've done it.'

'Yes, Miss.'

Claire climbed on to the chair and faced the window.

'All right, Claire?'

'Yes, Miss.'

'Go ahead, then.'

'I can't, Miss.'

'I see. And why can't you?'

'Kevin Jackson's staring at me through your window, Miss.'

'Then turn round and face the bookcase.'

'Yes, Miss.'

'There's nothing to stop you now, is there?'

'No, Miss.'

'Well, then?'

'I think the chair's too high, Miss.'

'Then bend your knees!'

'Yes, Miss.'

'I'm waiting, Claire.'

'I'b bitig by dose dow, Biss.'

'What did you say?'

'I'b bitig by dose, Biss.'

'Claire, get down from that chair this minute and stop playing silly games! I've had enough of it, do you hear?'

'Yed, Biss.'

'And stop biting your nose.'

'Yes, Miss.'

When Claire got down from the chair there were bite marks on her nose. She was close to tears.

Miss Hardstaff sighed. She ought, perhaps, to have a word with Claire's parents.

'Now listen to me, Claire. I want you to understand one simple thing. You can't bite your own nose. You can't bite it because . . . because it's too far away. Do you understand?'

'Yes, Miss.'

'Yes, Claire.'

'That's why I had to stand on the chair, Miss.'

'Standing on a chair doesn't make it easier to bite your nose, now does it?'

'Not unless I bend my knees like you said, Miss.'

'Claire, it is *not* easier to bite your nose if you bend your knees!'

'Only if I'm standing on a chair, Miss.'

'Claire, I've had quite enough of this. Just say that you're sorry to Anne and go back to your classroom. Well, young lady?'

'It's not fair, Miss. I was only showing you what Anne did. And it hurt, Miss.'

'I see. Anne, put those tissues away and tell me: did you or did you not bite your own nose?'

'It's still bleeding, Miss.'

'All right, keep the tissues.'

'Yes, Miss.'

'And did you bite your own nose?'

'No, Miss. I said I didn't.'

'No, Anne, I didn't think for one moment that you did.'

'I can't reach it, Miss.'

'Of course you can't reach it!'

'She stood on a chair, Miss.'

'Claire that's enough. You can't bite your own nose.'

'But I just showed you, Miss.'

'I don't know what you did, Claire, but believe me you did not bite your nose.'

'But, Miss . . .'

'And I don't wish to hear any more about it.'

'Miss?'

'Yes, Anne.'

'Kevin Jackson can.'

'Kevin Jackson can what, Anne?'

'Kevin Jackson can bite his nose, Miss. He's the only one in our class who can. I can't do it. I'm too small.' She glared across the room at Claire. 'Even standing on a chair, I'm too small.'

'Anne, I do *not* wish to hear one more word about noses or about biting. There's a school rule about biting and if anyone else bites anyone else they'll be sorry. Is that clear? Well, is it?'

'Yes, Miss.'

'Yes, Miss. Miss?'

'Don't say it, Claire, don't say it. There is to be no more biting—at all. Now back to your classrooms, both of you.'

'Yes, Miss.'

'Thank you, Miss. Miss?'

'Yes, Anne.'

'Shall I send Kevin Jackson to you?'

'I rather think not.'

'But, Miss, he'll be able to show—'

'Anne, I do not wish to see Kevin Jackson in my room EVER. Is that clear? Now go away.'

And who, she thought as the girls left, is Kevin Jackson? Of course, she knew all the children in the school. But Kevin Jackson? She would have to have a quick look at the admissions records. And as for that nonsense about biting noses! She had to put a stop to it before someone really hurt themselves. No, she thought, that's not it. Before someone really hurts someone else. She would have a word with the staff over coffee.

But, as well as the all-too-obvious teeth marks on Claire's nose when she got down from the chair, something else nagged uncomfortably at the back of her mind. It was only when she went downstairs for her coffee that she realized just how impossible it would have been for Kevin Jackson to look at Claire through her first floor study window.

Ruby

FLORENCE PARRY HEIDE

Ruby wanted to go over to Ethel's house to play. But Ruby's mother said, 'You have to watch Clyde.'

Clyde was Ruby's baby brother. He had just learned to walk.

'I don't want to watch Clyde. I want to go over to Ethel's house to play,' said Ruby.

Ruby's mother was tired. She had been watching Clyde all day. 'You have to watch Clyde because I have to take a bubble bath,' said Ruby's mother. She went into the bathroom.

Ruby called Ethel. 'I'll be over in a minute.'

Then Ruby watched Clyde.

She watched him take all of the clothes out of every chest of drawers in all of the rooms.

She watched him take all of the rice and all of the flour and all of the salt and all of the sugar and all of the coffee out of all of the kitchen cupboards and spill it all on the nice clean floor.

She watched him pull the tablecloth off the kitchen table. The bananas that had been on the table landed on Clyde's head.

Ruby watched Clyde start to cry very loud.

Her mother came out of the bathroom.

'What's going on?' she asked. 'I told you to watch Clyde.'

'I was watching him,' said Ruby truthfully. 'I was watching him the whole time.'

In a few minutes Ruby was ringing Ethel's doorbell. 'I told you I'd be over in a minute,' she said. 'I just had to watch Clyde.'

My Simple Little Brother

And The Great Aversion Therapy Experiment

LILITH NORMAN

There is no one in the whole wide world quite as stupid as my young brother, Fields. Fieldsy is seven now, and our sister, Lee, is sixteen. I'm almost in the middle, and my name is Paddy, short for Paddock. Our surname is Meadows, you see, and Dad gave us these names because he thinks he is some sort of funny man. Ha! ha!

But to get back to young Fieldsy. There is only one word for him: d-u-m-b. DUMB!

We first discovered this as soon as Fieldsy was old enough to talk—or to understand what other people were saying, which was even earlier. All little kids do some pretty weird things, and we used to think Fieldsy was just doing the normal strange experiments kids do as they try to find out what the world is all about and how things work. It was only when Fieldsy could talk

properly and let us know what passed for thought processes in that skull of his that we realized Fieldsy was blessed with a rich weirdness all his own.

For instance, Fieldsy was terrified of rain. I mean terrified! At the first drop he'd come hurtling inside at something faster than the speed of light and go to ground under his bed. Mum tried to drag him out and comfort him the first couple of dozen times, but Fieldsy just hooked his fingers through the bedsprings and clung on, screaming, 'No! No! No!'

'Leave him be,' said Dad crossly, as he watched Mum crawling about in the dust under the bed for what must have been the twenty-fifth time. 'Don't coddle the child. He'll grow out of it.'

It was only when Fieldsy was able to talk properly that we found out what the trouble was. It wasn't the noise of

the rain on the galvanized roof, as Lee had thought. (I could have told her that, and I did! Fieldsy reacted just the same even if the nearest galvanized roof was seventeen miles away.) No, it was something Dad had said when Fieldsy was only a toddler.

I can remember the long, dry summer we had had that year, but at last the clouds had banked up heavily in the southwest. You knew there was a corker of a storm coming—rain, hail, wind, the lot. Dad had got up from afternoon tea, cocked an eye at the weather, and said, in all innocence: 'I think I'll lock the hens into the shed early. It's going to rain buckets any minute now.'

That was Fieldsy's problem. As soon as the first drop hit him he had to hide away from the great deluge of buckets likely to clank down on his unprotected head. The fact that no buckets had yet fallen only made their likelihood even likelier in the next storm. Logic was never Fieldsy's strong point.

Do you need another example? There was the time Dad came home from the markets with a bulging wallet because he'd just sold a mob of heifers. The next thing he knew, the wallet was missing. So was Fieldsy. Dad found them together, naturally. Fieldsy was carefully pulling the notes out of the wallet one by one, and stuffing them down the drain outside the kitchen sink. Why? When Dad's face had changed back from stormy purple to pale mauve, that's what he wanted to know too.

It was so simple that only Fieldsy could have thought of it. Mum and Dad had been discussing what they would spend the money on. Mum had wanted a new washing-machine. Dad thought he might get the old sulky done up so that he could enter in the harness-horse section of the local show. Dad fancied himself a bit that way too, just as he fancied himself a comedian. In the end Mum had given in, with a very bad grace, and had said (her exact words): 'Well, if you want to throw your money down the drain, don't let me stop you!'

So Fieldsy was only trying to help. Of course, Dad had to take the drain apart, and Mum had to launder the notes. For a little while we were probably the only house in Australia with several hundred dollars pegged to our clothes line.

After that episode we all got stuck into Fieldsy. We tried to explain that a lot of the things that people say are only words: phrases that don't really mean what they seem to mean. Fieldsy listened to each of us in turn. Dad, Mum, Lee, and me. He frowned, he nodded his head, and once or twice he said crossly, '*I know that!*'

Heaven knows what was really going on in that bit of solid bone behind Fieldsy's face, for despite his agreement we didn't make any progress at all. In

fact it got worse, for Fieldsy now entered what we called his 'gruesome' phase.

It started a few weeks ago. We were having steak and kidney pudding for dinner. It looked luscious, with the steam rising from the white puddingy part—and the sort of smell that made you almost swoon at the thought of eating it. Mum served it up and started passing the plates round the table. Dad set his down, picked up his knife and fork, and inhaled with the sort of snort a horse makes when you drag it away from the trough.

'That is the best-looking steak and kidney pudding I've ever seen,' said Dad.

'It should be,' said Mum, smirking at Lee. 'It's a very special pudding, because Lee had a hand in making it.'

Well, that was enough for young Fieldsy. He turned white, then green. I was just passing him his plate, so I saw it all. Fieldsy just shook his head, clenched his teeth, and clamped his mouth shut tighter than a zipper. It didn't matter that Lee showed Fieldsy she still had two apparently normal hands. Maybe he thought she'd bought a plastic one and stuck it on, but he wouldn't touch the steak and kidney. Not that I worried, because I gobbled up his helping as well as my own. After all, if someone's dumb enough to turn down Mum's cooking . . . !

But it was the second bit of grue that led to the showdown. It might have been funny afterwards, but it certainly wasn't at the time. It started when Dad went to the sales to buy some bullocks, and this stray dog came running up, barking like a fool, just as Dad was driving the bullocks into the trailer. Bullocks went every which way, and in the flurry Dad got wedged against the side of the rails and broke his leg.

Mum was telling us all about it over dinner that night. 'It would never have happened if your father hadn't lost his head,' she said.

That did it. Fieldsy was off, weeping and carrying on a treat. Mum tried to explain that it was just a saying. Dad wasn't really lying in the hospital, one leg in plaster and no head to put on his pillow. It was no use. She just couldn't

get through to Dumb-bell. None of us could. Next day Fieldsy refused to go with us to visit Dad. Not that I blame him. I wouldn't like the idea of seeing a headless father lying about either.

But it was Dad's accident that led to 'the great aversion therapy experiment'. With Dad out of action, we needed someone to help run the farm, so Mum phoned Dad's brother, Uncle Percy. Uncle Percy was older than Dad, and the farm should have been his, but he had signed it all over to Dad and gone to the city to study. He said the only way to make anything of yourself these days was to get qualifications. Once you were qualified, the world was your oyster.

The trouble was, Uncle Percy was still getting qualified after thirty years. He even looked the part. Flared jeans, a T-shirt with POLITICIANS ARE MADE OF PLASTIC on the front of it, and stringy shoulder-length hair. (He's lucky there, because Dad is already as bald as Ayers Rock even though he's ten years younger than Uncle Percy.) The one thing wrong with Uncle Percy's gear was Uncle Percy—he's only about five foot six, and round as a keg—so he looked a bit odd.

But he certainly has qualifications. He has enough certificates and degrees and diplomas to sink a fair-sized fleet, but there is always one more he had to

get 'just to make sure'. He's a fully-qualified vet, and a Doctor of Philosophy; a fitter and turner, an archaeologist, and an expert on conchology. He's got diplomas in agriculture and town planning, and a commercial pilot's licence; he's studied wine-making and Ancient Egyptian and psychology, and dozens of other things. It was that last bit that was to prove our downfall, though. Psychology.

As soon as Uncle Percy arrived he insisted we all go to see Dad for 'a family conference'. So Mum had to explain about young Fieldsy and his distorted view of the world. It took her three hours by the time she remembered *all* Fieldsy's idiocies!

'Stuff and nonsense,' snorted Uncle Percy. 'You're handling the boy all wrong. What you should use is aversion therapy.'

We all looked blank except Fieldsy— he was playing outside.

So Uncle Percy explained what aversion therapy was. 'It's the treatment they use on alcoholics,' he said. I could see Mum beginning to clench her teeth, a sure sign she was getting mad. I guess it is upsetting to have your darling youngest son discussed as though he is really sick, even when he is a bit strange in the head. Uncle Percy ploughed on regardless. 'What they do

is give the subject an electric shock every time he starts to take a drink.'

'You are *not* going to give *my* son electric shocks!' snapped Mum.

Uncle Percy saw the glint in her eye and backtracked hastily. 'No, no. Nothing as drastic as that. But don't you see, it's just because the things Fields expects to happen never *do* happen that he persists in his—er— delusion? Now, if he could once have one of these silly phrases come true I think the shock would snap him out of it for good. It's what he *imagines* that is so much worse than what he would actually see.'

Well, we argued back and forth for another hour or so, and at last Mum agreed. But only on condition that there would be absolutely no electric shocks, and no physical damage of any sort. She didn't seem to worry so much about mental damage, but I did. After all, there's not much between Fieldsy's ears, and what there is seems pretty precariously balanced to me. Anyway, it was finally agreed that the great aversion therapy experiment would take place the next day, as soon as Uncle Percy had bought the necessary equipment. I agreed to be the muggins who would start it all off.

The next day was a Saturday, and straight after lunch I went into action. I took Fieldsy aside and put on my

solemnest face. 'Now, you've got to be especially good while Uncle Percy is here,' I said. 'No mucking up. Because whatever you do, Uncle Percy will know. *He's got eyes in the back of his head!*'

Fieldsy stared at me, his jaw slowly sinking down like a faulty pump-handle. 'Gee!' he whispered at last, as the wonder of Uncle Percy's physical endowment gradually sank in.

'Sure,' I said. 'Didn't you know that?' Fieldsy shook his head dumbly. 'Well, if you don't believe me, sneak out and have a look. He's out on the verandah having a doze.'

Fieldsy stared at me for a long minute. Then he turned and tiptoed to the verandah where Uncle Percy had planted himself as planned. Fieldsy sneaked up behind him. Uncle Percy had let his head fall forward on to his chest so that Fieldsy could have a good look at the back of his head. Fieldsy's hand inched out, paused, inched on, until he was just touching Uncle Percy's long black locks. He turned then to look at me and I nodded encouragingly. Fieldsy turned back and began to part Uncle Percy's hair.

Suddenly he froze. His hands clenched and he gave a sort of ultrasonic yip. There were two great china eyes staring at him. Then everything happened at once. Fieldsy, his hands still clenched in terror, turned to run. There was a tattering tear, like the sound of a sheet of sticking plaster being ripped off a table top, and the whole of Uncle Percy's hair came away. As it jerked free the strands of hair bounced apart again, showing those two staring, china-white eyes. Fieldsy thought they were coming after him. He gave another strangled yip and flung his hands over *his* eyes to blot out the horrible sight. The inside of the wig, still well-covered with adhesive, transferred itself to Fieldsy's forehead and stuck there back to front, with Uncle Percy's locks covering Fieldsy's face like a veil.

All this time Uncle Percy was screeching like a jet taking off in a bottle. And me? I just stood there, solidified. At first I thought Uncle Percy had been well and truly scalped. It was only when the hair stuck fast to Fieldsy that the penny dropped and I realized the old phony had been wearing a wig all along.

Meanwhile Fieldsy, finding himself enveloped in fronds of hairy darkness, turned and floundered his way to the back door. Once outside he took off across the paddock towards town. Perhaps he thought that if he could run far enough and fast enough he could get away from whatever was trying to swallow him. By the time I had unfrozen and reached the back door myself, Fieldsy was half-way across the paddock.

Near the fowl yard he fell over the chopping block, and he covered about twenty yards on his hands and knees before his own momentum brought him back to his feet. Unfortunately the hens saw him—a four-legged *something* with a mask of black hair scuttling towards them. The hens, being even less well-balanced mentally than Fieldsy, panicked.

'Fo-o—x! Fox-fox-fox!' they shrieked, and headed for the highest branches they could find, lurching upwards with straining wings and a shower of falling feathers. (The shock turned them all off the lay for a month.)

Fieldsy kept on going.

His way lay right in line with the weedy little creek that formed our boundary, but nothing could stop him now. He plunged into the creek, went under briefly, came up spluttering, and splashed across. The wig was now plastered flat to his face, in strands, like the slats of a picket fence, and the china eyeballs clonked on his cheekbones. Chickweed and mud hung all about him.

Then he hit the highway into town, and the feel of the firm asphalt let him put on an extra burst of speed. It was only half a mile into town and Fieldsy covered it in record time. The main street was deserted. All the adults were at home, all the kids were at the pictures. The only shop open was the milk bar beside the pictures.

As Fieldsy reached the milk bar he was slowing down. He was puffing hard, and he had to limit himself to a fast walk. Mick, the owner of the milk bar, was lounging at the entrance, waiting for the rush of kids at interval, when he saw Fieldsy coming, and came out to help him.

'Whatsamatter, kid?' he asked, grabbing Fieldsy by the arm. Fieldsy, certain the monster had caught him at last, tore himself free and fled into the nearest doorway to hide. It happened to be the cinema.

He blundered on, through one door and then another. He tore down the aisle, found his way up the stairs to the stage, and teetered along in front of the screen. He was puffing and blowing even more now, and giving little grunting calls for help. For a few minutes he was silhouetted against the screen: a faceless, gibbering *thing*, with great staring white eyeballs gleaming in

the light from the projector, a second pair of smaller beady eyeballs (his own) just above them, and with horrible dripping tentacles.

It was unfortunate that the film he interrupted was *Slime Man from Saturn*, for the audience gave one unanimous scream of terror, rose to their feet with a crashing up of seats, and fled in all directions.

It took quite a while to collect them all and herd them back into the theatre. Even when they saw what the monster really was, some of them refused to go

back. A few of the more timid ones have never gone to the pictures again.

I reached the theatre just as kids and adults shot out every which way. There was no sign of Fieldsy, but I felt somehow that the uproar must have something to do with him. I fought my way in against the tide, and found Fieldsy sitting in the front row of the stalls enjoying the film. The water from the creek had finally softened the glue on the wig and it had fallen off. Fieldsy, free at last, and rather startled to find himself at the pictures, had decided to

take advantage of his good fortune, for Mum never lets him go to horror films.

When Fieldsy and I got home (with the wig, which I found lying on the stage) Uncle Percy took it without a word. Mum offered to put it through the washing-machine, but Uncle Percy just took it away and hid it at the bottom of his suitcase. He goes around in his scalp now, and he looks better for it. He's even talking seriously of getting a job and putting some of his many qualifications to work. After his aversion therapy experiment he's beginning to feel that all theory and no practice may not be enough.

And Fieldsy? Did the great aversion therapy experiment work? Well, I'll let you figure that out for yourself. But if you want to know what the gruesome little monster is doing right this minute, I'll tell you. He's down in the paddock with my fat old pony, Skimble, watching him like a hawk. Why? Because Dad said at breakfast this morning that all Skimble does these days is stand around eating his head off.

Why Cows Don't Fly

TRADITIONAL

Leaving Ebeltoft church one Sunday, Peter and Gunnar walked down to the bay.

'You know,' said Peter, 'it's very odd.'

'What is?'

'About the birds. I often wonder about the birds.'

Gunnar eyed the gulls patrolling the shoreline. 'What about them? They're just birds, that's all.'

'No, well, the preacher always talks about the ways of God being mysterious. What I can't understand is how birds get to fly.'

'They fly because they're birds,' said Gunnar. 'That's what birds do. They wouldn't be birds if they didn't.'

'No, what I mean is birds are little. They don't need very much. Yet God gave them wings and they can fly all over the place to get what they want.'

'That's true enough,' said Gunnar, watching the gulls.

'Now, cows are much bigger. They have to eat all the time. Yet here they are, stuck on the ground.'

At that moment something splashed on Gunnar's upturned face.

'I just don't understand it,' Peter went on. He was looking out over the bay.

Gunnar wiped his face on his sleeve.

'Peter,' he said, 'I think I know why God in his wisdom didn't give wings to the cow.'

Spider's Surprise

Sarah Morcom

Old Mag the hag was a witch. She was very old and ugly with a runny eye and a moustache, and you could smell her coming a mile off. Old Mag lived in a dreadful cottage called The Dumps. (The name suited it very well.)

Also in The Dumps lived Black Bert. Black Bert was the fattest, hairiest, dirtiest spider in the neighbourhood and he lived in a dark corner of Old Mag's kitchen. He thought he was very important and bullied all the other spiders so they were afraid of him. All day long he sat lazily on his filthy web, giving orders and surveying his domain like a fat king. Sometimes he would sidle off on his hairy legs to take up position by the front door, where he acted as chief bouncer, frightening off any creepy-crawly that dared to go near (and usually eating it afterwards). Old Mag had a soft spot for Black Bert. She let him ride around on her hat occasionally, which he thought was a great treat, and he particularly enjoyed crawling behind her ear.

One day, Old Mag bought a magazine. It was called *WITCH—The Mag for the Modern Hag*. She sat down and put on her smeary spectacles to read it.

''Ere, wot's she readin'?' croaked Black Bert, who was a nosy old spider. 'Go 'n' 'ave a look, will yer.' He ordered one of the young spiders to go and spy on Old Mag to see what she was reading.

The young spider let himself nimbly down on his thread over Old Mag's head. But what he saw on the page nearly made him fall on to Old Mag's lap in fright. It read:

SPIDER SOUFFLÉ ~ A NEW REMEDY FOR THE AGEING WITCH

Capture your lost youth with this delicious tonic ~ tasty and effective ~ Knocks years off your life!

INGREDIENTS

One fully matured spider (as large and juicy as possible)
Two tablespoonfuls medium-sized spiders
½ teaspoon money spiders
¾ pint slug Slime

The young spider read no further—he had seen enough to make him feel most uncomfortable. He quickly returned to Black Bert, quite sure they were going to be eaten.

'Nah, she ain't gonna cook us, stupid,' growled Black Bert. 'She'll use them imported ones from outside.'

Black Bert sounded very sure, but underneath he was really quite frightened, because they all knew that imported spiders were thought to be tough and tasteless.

The next day, further alarming things began to happen. Old Mag seemed to be in a very strange mood. She pottered round the cottage tidying things up, and even dusted away some of the larger cobwebs. Black Bert was furious at this disturbance to his filthy home. At tea time Old Mag did something unbelievable for her—she washed her hair! I won't tell you what sort of things came out of it into the water (it might put you off your next meal), but the sink was blocked for days afterwards. Then the spiders watched, amazed, as she laid the table for two with her best black china and a vase of deadly nightshade and stinkweed as a centrepiece. That evening a young, rather greasy-looking wizard called at The Dumps, and he and Old Mag sat down to a candle-lit dinner. They leered at each other and held hands across the table, and Black Bert didn't like it one bit.

Over the next few days the young wizard visited very often. Old Mag seemed to have forgotten about Black Bert altogether. She no longer asked him to ride on her hat and instead spent all her time dressing up and making herself look fancy for her wizard boyfriend. All this put Black Bert in a nasty temper and he took it out on the younger spiders, making their lives a daily misery.

Then, one morning, one of Black Bert's spies came rushing to him in a state of extreme panic. 'She's got the spider recipe out again and the pot's already on the boil. We're done for now!'

Black Bert thought quickly. 'All right you lot, keep yer 'eads on. This calls for Emergency Operations. Go 'n' get the Black Box an' don't mess about!'

Only Black Bert knew what was in the Black Box. On it was printed TOP SECRET in large letters. Black Bert took a rusty old key and opened it up. Inside was a large package marked CAUTION: OPEN IN EMERGENCY ONLY. With the package was a dirty sheet of paper covered with spidery writing. It read:

SPIDER SUPERGLUE: THE ULTIMATE DEFENSIVE WEAPON FOR SPIDERS
1 Eat as much of enclosed confectionery as possible
2 Spin webs in normal way

Black Bert ripped open the parcel and there, in a sticky, glistening pile, was an enormous quantity of wine gums.

'Right, mates,' said Black Bert. 'Get stuck into this lot and FAST!'

Immediately the pile of wine gums was covered with a wriggling mass of spiders, all tearing and chomping at the sweets. Black Bert sat in the middle, dribbling and smacking his lips in an unsavoury manner.

When they'd finished, the spiders felt very full, and extremely sticky.

'Now then, comrades,' said Black Bert with a loud belch. 'Back to your stations and get spinnin'!'

Meanwhile Old Mag was getting the pot nice and hot for the Spider Soufflé. She read the recipe out loud to herself: 'One fully-matured spider—Ah yes . . .'

She went over to the dark corner where Black Bert lived, with a nasty smile on her face. 'Bertie! Bertie, darling. How would you fancy a little ride on Auntie Mag's hat today? Come out, dearie, and say hello to your Auntie.'

Black Bert bounced back into the shadows, grinning a horrible grin. Old Mag poked at him with her finger and immediately a mass of sticky web stuck to it. (Black Bert's web was made of Spider superglue!)

Old Mag pulled the curtain aside and got quite a shock—the curtain stuck to her hand! She pulled hard but it wouldn't budge.

Old Mag stamped her foot and muttered some nasty words under her breath. Finally she gave a great yank and brought the curtain pole clanging down. She fell back on to a chair, cursing and grumbling, and in his corner Black Bert sat smiling and rubbing his hairy front legs together in a quiet satisfaction.

Meanwhile, the other spiders had been weaving their superglue webs with great speed all over the kitchen, covering every piece of furniture they could find. So when Old Mag tried to get up, she found the chair stuck firmly to her bottom. At that moment, the doorbell rang and Black Bert slunk away to answer it. It was Old Mag's boyfriend and he was just in time to see Old Mag give a last, furious tug at the chair, ripping her skirt off with it. There she stood in her baggy, black bloomers, showing her horrible, warty legs. I'm afraid to say she looked so ridiculous that the wizard couldn't stop himself laughing.

Old Mag was so angry it looked as if she would burst—her face was purple. 'Get out!' she screamed at the wizard. 'Get out! And you needn't come back again!'

Then she turned to Black Bert. 'I think this is all your doing, you creepy little insect. Get rid of this stuff immediately or I'll turn you into—into—'

'Spider Soufflé?' said Black Bert with a leery smile. 'That's wot you was goin' to turn us all into, wasn't it, *dear* Auntie Mag? And until you promise to leave us alone an' treat us respec'ful-like, I'm afraid you'll 'ave a sticky time of it.'

'All right, I promise, I promise,' said Old Mag, dragging the rug with her. (She'd stuck to that now.)

By the time all the spiders had mixed the special paste to unstick the superglue, Old Mag looked like a walking scrapyard, with half her kitchen stuck to her. She didn't get rid of the wizard as quickly as she would have liked either, for in trying to get out, he'd stuck to the doorhandle.

So that is how Black Bert showed Old Mag he was not going to be made into Spider Soufflé and ruled the kitchen once more. Mag went back to her old, dirty ways again, but she was always very polite to any spider she saw, for fear of meeting a sticky end!

The Amazing Talking Pig

MICK GOWAR

It was a cold autumn night on Brown's Farm. Mr Brown, the farmer, had finished washing up his supper things, and was just settling down in his comfy armchair to read his library book, when there was a gentle *Tap-tappity-tap* on the front door.

'Bother!' muttered Mr Brown, grumpily. 'I was just getting comfortable.'

He looked at the clock on the mantelpiece: it was half-past nine. 'Who can that be, so late?' he wondered.

Cautiously, Mr Brown opened the door and looked out. There was no one there. He was just closing the door when he heard a cough. Mr Brown peered out into the darkened farmyard; there was still no one there. He started to close the door again.

'Ah-hem, ah-*hem!*' said a voice.

It seemed to be coming from the step. Mr Brown looked down and saw, to his astonishment, a small pink pig.

'Hullo,' said the pig, politely.

'WAAAH!' yelled Mr Brown, staggering back.

'I said: Hullo,' repeated the pig.

'You . . . you . . . you . . . can . . .' spluttered Mr Brown.

'. . . come in?' suggested the pig. 'Thanks very much. I will.'

And it walked past Mr Brown and into the warm cosy sitting room.

'Wow!' exclaimed the pig, looking round the room. 'This is some sty!' It sniffed the carpet. 'And *that* is what I call High Class Straw!'

Mr Brown tottered unsteadily into the room.

'But . . . but . . . but,' he gasped, 'you can . . . can . . .'

'. . . sit down and make myself at home?' suggested the pig. 'Ta, very much!'

With a quick spring it jumped into Mr Brown's armchair.

'*Very* nice!' said the pig, snuggling down into the cushions. 'And what's this—?'

It sniffed Mr Brown's library book, which he'd left open on the chair. 'Oooh! I see I'm just in time for a snack,' said the pig, licking its lips. 'Goody!' And it tore out a page and began chewing.

'Not bad,' said the pig thoughtfully, as it swallowed the page. 'I prefer a little warm swill, myself, but if this is all you've got in the house to eat, who am I to complain?'

'You can . . . you can . . . *talk!*' Mr Brown finally managed to stammer out.

'*Oh, brilliant!*' said the pig sarcastically. 'Of course I can talk, what do you think I am, thick or something?'

'No, no, no,' replied Mr Brown hastily. 'It's just that

. . . well . . . but . . . but you've never spoken to *me* before.'

'Haven't needed to,' explained the pig. 'Everything was OK until now. Nice food, clean straw, cosy sty, good conversation with the other pigs—what more could a pig want? But tonight? *Brrrr!* That sty is *not* the place to spend a cold night, I can tell you. Talk about freezing? I was colder than a penguin's bottom!

'So I said to myself: *Horatio*—that's my name, by the way—*Horatio*, I said, *this is the time of year when a pig needs a warm fire, a cup of hot cocoa, and a proper bed with plenty of warm blankets.* So here I am.'

Mr Brown shook his head in amazement.

The pig suddenly looked worried. 'You do *have* cocoa, don't you?' it asked.

'Er . . . yes . . .' replied Mr Brown.

'Great!' said the pig. 'I like two sugars. Oh, and don't let the milk boil. I can't *stand* skin on my cocoa.'

Mr Brown walked out to the kitchen like a robot in shock. He opened the fridge and, as if in a dream, he poured a pint of milk into a saucepan and put it on the hotplate.

As he waited for the milk to heat, Mr Brown tried to get used to the idea of his amazing guest.

'Fantastic!' he said to himself. 'Unbelievable! A talking pig! I've never heard of anything like it before. I'm sure it must be the only talking pig in the whole world . . .'

'Yoo-hoo! Mr Brown!' called the pig from the sitting room. 'Don't forget what I said: no skin on my cocoa, please.'

Mr Brown poured the cocoa into two cups—one for him, one for the pig. Then he had second thoughts, and poured the pig's cocoa into a bigger cup. Then he had third thoughts, and poured a large whisky into his cocoa. (He'd had a nasty shock; he needed a little something.)

'The only one in the whole world . . .' thought Mr Brown, as the whisky glugged into his cup. 'This could make me famous! I can see the headlines in all the papers: FARMER BROWN AND HIS AMAZING TALKING PIG! I'll be on radio and TV, too! That pig could make me rich! That pig could make me a millionaire! I'd better be very nice to that pig.'

'Here you are,' said Mr Brown, putting the pig's cocoa down in front of the fire. 'And if you want anything else, anything at all—just tell me . . .'

By midnight, Mr Brown bitterly regretted his promise to give the pig anything it wanted. There seemed to be nothing that the pig *didn't* want. Mr Brown had never had to work so hard in all his life.

First, the pig had wanted a second cup of cocoa. Then the pig had asked for a snack.

'A *proper* one this time, please!'

So Mr Brown had made up a special warm mash to the pig's favourite recipe. The pig had sat in the armchair yelling out orders, while Mr Brown scurried frantically in the kitchen.

'Two jars of strawberry jam—large ones—and one tin of treacle. Now, crumble in sixteen Weetabix—got that?'

'Er, yes . . .' Mr Brown had replied, desperately crumbling Weetabix as fast as he could.

'Now mix up four pounds of creamed potatoes—fresh, mind, none of that powdered rubbish—and use *real* butter. Humans may not be able to tell the difference between margarine and butter, but pigs can! And when you've creamed the potatoes, add two jars of marmalade—the expensive sort, with big chunks of orange peel. Then two jars of Marmite, three pounds of stewed prunes. And finally, two tablespoons of Double Strength Madras Curry Powder—for that extra tingle, know what I mean?'

After its meal, the pig demanded a bubble bath, in the old tin tub in front of the fire.

'I can't stand cold bathrooms,' the pig had explained.

Poor Mr Brown. He'd had to run between the kitchen and the sitting room with pots and pans and kettles of hot water. Then he'd had to mix up a bubble bath using two giant containers of washing-up liquid and a bottle of very expensive after-shave his sister Lydia had given him for his birthday.

Mr Brown was now weak with tiredness. The pig wasn't.

'Let's have some music,' said the pig. 'I see you've got a banjo. Let's have a sing-song!'

So Mr Brown played the banjo until his fingertips were sore and throbbing, while the pig sang every song that Mr Brown knew in the most awful squealing tenor voice that Mr Brown had ever heard. The pig also changed all the words so that all the songs were about pigs. Its favourite songs were: 'Old MacDonald Had A Pig' and 'All Pigs Bright And Beautiful'.

'I'm beginning to feel a little sleepy,' said the pig, when it had finished singing.

Mr Brown breathed a huge sigh of relief.

'So, time for a bed-time story—or two!' announced the pig.

Bleary-eyed and sore-throated, Mr Brown stumbled through *The Three Little Pigs* and *The Three Billy Goats Gruff*—but with the goats changed to pigs, of course.

'Well,' said the pig, eventually, 'time for bed—I mustn't miss my beauty sleep. Where's my room?'

Mr Brown led the way upstairs, and into the guest bedroom.

'Oh, dear,' said the pig, inspecting the bed. 'Tut-tut! This is no good—the bed's too narrow, and the mattress is much too lumpy. I'll have to sleep in your bed.'

Wearily, Mr Brown led the way to his own room.

'Not bad,' said the pig, snuggling under the covers. 'But still not perfect.'

'What's the matter *now*?' groaned Mr Brown.

'No hotty-totty,' replied the pig.

'No *what*?' asked Mr Brown.

'No hot-water bottle,' said the pig. 'You don't want me to catch cold, do you?'

Mr Brown staggered downstairs to fetch the hot-water bottle.

'And I forgot, I'll need a drink of water, too,' the pig said as Mr Brown came back into the room.

With a weary groan Mr Brown fetched a bowl of water.

'Now a good-night kiss . . .' said the pig, puckering its snout.

'Do I have to?' asked Mr Brown.

'Yes,' said the pig, 'you do!'

Mr Brown woke up. He was still in his armchair. The fire was out, and the morning light was glinting through a thin crack between his curtains. His library book had fallen face down on the floor at his feet. He looked at the clock on the mantelpiece: it was half-past seven.

The pig!

Mr Brown sat up, horrified. Then he chuckled to himself. It had all been a dream. He must have fallen asleep in his chair and dreamt the whole thing!

Mr Brown got to his feet and stretched. Then he bent down and began to rake out the cold ashes of his fire.

'WAAAAH!' yelled Mr Brown, as something wet and snout-like tapped him on the back of the neck.

'Good morning!' said the cheerful, snuffly voice behind him. 'What's for breakfast? I'm ravenous!'

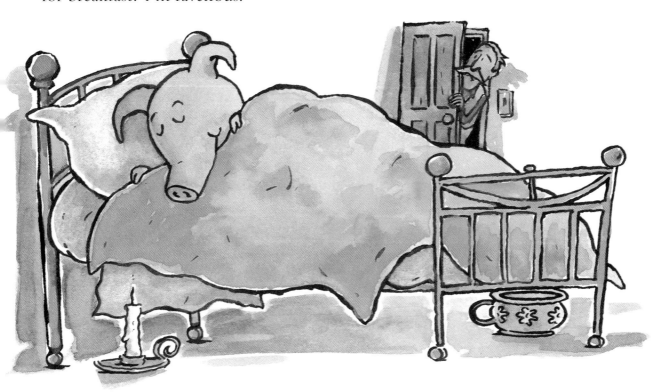

The Old Mule Won't Work

RICHARD AND JUDY DOCKREY YOUNG

There was an old man and his grandson who lived in an old cabin out in the woods, all by theirselves. The boy was kind of lazy, but he was a good boy. One day the old man said to his grandson, 'Go on down there to that barn and hitch up that old mule and go plough the north forty.'

The boy kind of dragged on down to the barn, and the mule was standing there with his head down in the hay. But he wasn't eating, he was watching the grandson. The grandson come up there, and he said, 'OK, mule, let's go!'

The old mule jerked his head up in the air, and said, 'You go and tell your granddaddy that I ain't going 'o work today!'

Well, the boy, he let out a scream and run back up to the house and said, 'Granddaddy, Granddaddy, that mule done told me he ain't a-going 'o work today!'

The granddaddy looked at him and said, 'You go tell that mule that I said he was going 'o work today.'

Well, the grandson, he kind of bit his lip, and gulped a few times, and he

went back down there. The old mule was a-watching him real close. The boy got down there and said, 'Mule, Granddad said you was going 'o work today.'

The old mule threw his head up and kicked around a little bit, and said, 'You go and tell your granddaddy I said I wasn't going 'o work today!'

The boy run back up to the house and said, 'Granddaddy, that mule says he ain't a-going 'o work today!'

Well, the granddaddy, he's done figured out that the boy, he just doesn't want 'o work. So he says, 'Well, I'll go tell that blamed mule myself!' So, he took his cane down off the wall, and he called his little black dog and he hobbled on down the hill to where that mule was, with his grandson a-following behind him a-trembling.

The old man come up close onto the mule: old mule had his head down like he was eating, but he wasn't really. Granddaddy walked right up and rapped the mule on the hoof with that cane and he said, 'Now, mule, I said you's going 'o plough!'

That old mule he throwed up his head, and he let out a yowl, and he said, 'I told you I wasn't going 'o work today!'

Well, Granddaddy, he let out a scream, and he run just as hard as he could run with his little old black dog behind him. He run, and he run, plumb past the house out into the woods. He found hisself a stump, and he sat down, a-panting hard. He was sitting there, wiping sweat, and the little old black dog ran up next to him.

The man was sitting there, puffing and panting, and he said, 'If'n that don't beat all I've ever heard!'

And the little black dog looked up and said, 'Yeah, me too!'

Wolves 11 Rabbits 0

DAVID HENRY WILSON

Hi there. Wolfie's the name. Mine, that is, not yours. (Unless yours happens to be Wolfie, too.) I'm the famous Wolfie that got unfairly and rather fatally killed by Red Riding Hood's grandma. You remember the story? Well, if you don't, too bad, because I'm not going to tell it to you. I've told that story so many times, I'm beginning to believe it's true.

No, this is a football story. We forest animals are crazy about football. Find a clearing, and you'll find two teams kicking a coconut. And what teams we've produced! Who hasn't heard of Monkeyster United, Assenal, Leoparpool, Toadenham Hotspawn? But the greatest team of all was without doubt The Wolves. And the greatest day of the greatest team was without doubt the day when we won the Forest Animals (F.A.) Cup.

Modesty forbids me to mention that I was the captain. Well, I suppose I could mention it. I was the captain.

What a day that was! Of course, the F.A. Cup was the biggest competition in the forest. Maybe it still is. After Red Riding Hood's granny put four bullets in me, I kind of lost interest in football. In fact, I kind of lost interest in everything. But back in the good old pre-granny days, I just lived for football. And the proudest day of my life was when I led the team to victory in the F.A. Cup.

Forest football rules were the same as ordinary football rules except for one additional law: any player caught eating a member of the other side was automatically sent off. In the days when the good old days were not so good, there were a lot of sendings-off. There was one famous occasion during

the grim winter of '78 when a third-round match between ourselves and the ducks ended with only the referee on the field. The match was abandoned as a draw, and the ducks never showed up for the replay.

Anyway I was telling you about the year we won the cup. And in particular, I want to tell you about the Cup Final. And particularly in particular, I want to tell you about the brilliant strategy that won us the cup. Under my captaincy, incidentally. Did I mention that I was captain?

We were due to play the rabbits, and we all knew we were in for a tough match. The rabbits had already won the cup two years running—and I mean running. Their main advantage was sheer speed. They were so fast that it always looked as if there were fifty of them on the field. Some of us reckoned there *were* fifty of them on the field. There might only have been eleven at the start, but you know how quick rabbits are at multiplying. Anyway, they were hot favourites to win, and we were the underdogs—or underwolves— or whatever you'd like to call us. Team morale was very low.

'We haven't got a chance,' moaned Wilfie, our goalkeeper. 'Look what they did to us last year.'

'What did they do to us last year?' I asked, pretending that it had slipped my memory.

'They beat us 47–0,' he groaned.

'Maybe you had an off day,' I suggested.

'Wilfie was the only one of us who touched the ball,' said Willy, our striker. 'Apart from me kicking off.'

'And then I was only picking it out of the back of the net,' said Wilfie.

'But that was *last* year,' I said, trying to lift their spirits.

'What's different this year?' asked our left wing.

'You've got me as captain,' I said.

'And what difference is that going to make?' asked our right wing.

Well, I couldn't really tell him. You don't expect that sort of question out of the blue.

I did what I could to encourage the team, but by the end of that training session, they'd convinced themselves that they'd be lucky to lose 50–0.

'Think positive,' I said. 'If we do as well as last year, it'll only be 47–0.'

But they wouldn't listen.

When I got home, my wife noticed that I wasn't my usual cheerful self.

'What's the matter with you?' she asked. 'You look as if you've just been invited to the woodcutters' ball.'

My wife was very sensitive to my feelings. I told her the problem.

'Ugh, ugh,' she said. 'You and your football. It's only a game, isn't it?'

My wife didn't know very much about football.

'A game?' I said. 'A GAME? It's the F.A. Cup Final!'

'Isn't that a game?' she asked.

Patiently, I explained to her just what the F.A. Cup Final was.

'It still sounds like a game to me,' she said.

Talking to my wife was about as up-cheering as talking to our goalkeeper. I gave my eldest cub a cuff round the ear for breathing and then lay down in the corner of the cave to work out tactics. The only tactic I could think of was to pull a muscle on the morning of the match.

'I wouldn't have thought rabbits would be a problem,' said my wife later that night.

'That's because you haven't seen them play,' I said.

'Why don't you just eat them?' she suggested.

'Because,' I said witheringly, 'it's against the rules.'

'What rules?'

Once again I delivered a patient explanation.

'Hm,' she said, when I'd finished, 'no problem.'

'What do you mean, no problem?' I asked.

'Leave it all to me,' she said.

'But you don't know anything about football!' I cried.

'Who needs to know about football?'

she replied. 'You'll have your silly little cup, and then perhaps the rest of us can have some peace and quiet.'

Now, when my wife said she'd do something, she always did it, but how even she could turn a 50–0 defeat into victory was beyond my imagination. And then she told me her plan.

'You couldn't!' I said.

'I can,' she said. 'And I will.'

'It's not possible,' I said.

'You'll see,' she said.

The next day after breakfast—my wife didn't have any breakfast; she said she had to get into training right away—I took her along to the ground and showed her round.

'No problem,' she said again, 'so long as you're sure of the rules.'

'Sure I'm sure of the rules,' I said.

'In that case,' she said, 'the cup's yours.'

From that moment on, I had no doubts, but I didn't tell my team about the plan. Careless talk costs cups. I just laughed at their pessimism, astonished them with my confidence, and laid in a stock of goodies for our winners' party. They thought I was mad.

'Wolfie's gone goofy!' said Willy.

'50–0!' moaned Wilfie. 'And he's throwing a party!'

'Trust in your captain,' I said with the quiet authority of the born leader. 'The cup's as good as ours.'

At last the great day dawned. My wife was to make her own way to the ground, so I took the cubs and installed them on the terrace, where they had a vital part to play. Then I strolled into our changing room.

'50–0!' moaned Wilfie, our goal-keeper. 'I shall be the howling stock of the forest.'

'There's no point in our going out there,' said Willy, our striker. 'Let's strike.'

'Oh, ye of little faith!' I cried. 'I've told you we can't lose. Now, get ready to inspect the pitch.'

'Inspect the graveyard, more like it!' mumbled Wilfie.

Kick off was at 3 p.m. At 2 p.m. precisely, I led my team out to inspect the pitch. A loud cheer came from our supporters. These were my eight cubs—no other wolves had bothered to turn up. Who wants to see their team get beaten 50–0? From the millions of rabbits on the other side of the ground there were loud boos, which turned into cheers and a thumping of hind legs as the rabbit team came bounding on to the pitch.

'All ready for the slaughter, Wolfie?' mocked the rabbit captain.

'Ho ho, very funny, Bunny,' I said. 'But you'll soon be laughing on the other side of your bobtail.'

'Ha ha,' said Captain Rabbit. 'You must be the joker in the pack.'

'And I suppose you're the wit of the warren,' I replied, quick as a flash.

It was a clear verbal victory to me, even though he did slightly spoil it with some idiotic remark about me being the half-wit of the wolf-asylum. Then he led his team off one way, and I led mine off the other.

Before we disappeared into our changing room, I gave a secret signal to the cubs. At once they set up what I must confess was a rather unconvincing chant of 'We are the champions!' Unconvincing, but it did the trick. At once there was a storm of booing from the other side, and then a million rabbit voices began to sing their special football song 'You'll never walk alone'. It was an essential part of our plan. The louder they sang, the less they'd hear.

At 2.55 p.m. I led my team back on to the field. By now the ground was full—almost entirely of rabbits. With typical lack of sportsmanship they booed us all the way, but then they gradually fell silent as they waited for their heroes to come on to the pitch.

They had a long wait.

'Where are they?' growled Boris the Bear, who had been made referee because no one would argue with him.

'No idea,' I lied. 'Maybe they're scared of being beaten.'

All eyes were now turned towards the rabbits' changing room, but there was

not a sound or a movement from there.

'If they don't hurry up,' said Boris, 'I shall award the match to The Wolves.'

'Oh, good heavens!' I said. 'What an absolutely dreadful idea!'

'Has anybody seen them?' bawled the bear, getting more and more sore-headed.

'Well, yes, we all have,' I replied. 'They were here half an hour ago, trying to frighten us off. Shall I go and see what they're doing?'

'Yes!' yelled the bear. 'And be quick about it!'

'Of course I will, sir,' I said, and trotted across the field.

I stopped outside the rabbits' door, and my voice rang out loud and clear through the hushed arena:

'Come along, my dears! The referee's waiting to start our game! We don't want to keep him waiting!'

There was no reply.

'Open the door!' roared Boris the Bear.

Obediently I opened the door.

'Well, fancy that!' I exclaimed. 'There's nobody here!'

A gasp of astonishment rabbited round the arena.

'There is absolutely nobody here!' I repeated. 'The little devils have run away. And they've even left the back door open!'

Indeed the changing room was completely empty. The only sign of our opponents was an odd ball of rabbit fur dotted around the floor.

'That's it!' roared Boris. 'No rabbits, no game. I award the cup to The Wolves.'

It was a proud day for me. Captain of the side that won the cup. My team mates carried me shoulder-high off the field. One or two spectators complained, of course, but since both teams had been on the field, and had been seen going back to their separate changing rooms, it was clear that no rules had been broken. No one could blame us if the rabbits had, so to speak, chickened out.

Our party went on all night and most of the next day. We had achieved the greatest upset in sporting history since the tortoise had beaten the hare. It was a pity my wife wasn't able to join in the celebrations, but I explained to my team that she didn't really like football very much. Besides, she was suffering from a bad attack of indigestion.

Wishes

NATALIE BABBITT

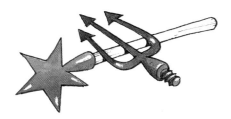

One day when things were dull in Hell, the Devil fished around in his bag of disguises, dressed himself as a fairy godmother, and came up into the World to find someone to bother. He wandered down the first country road he came to and before long he met a crabby farm wife stumping along with a load of switches on her back.

'Good morning, my dear,' said the Devil in his best fairy-godmother voice. 'It's a fine day, isn't it?'

'It's not,' said the farm wife. 'There hasn't been a fine day in the World in twenty years.'

'That long?' said the Devil.

'That long,' she snapped.

Now, it was the Devil's plan that morning to make a nuisance of himself by granting wishes, and he decided there was no time like now to begin. 'See here then,' he said to the farm wife. 'I will grant you one wish—anything at all—and that ought to cheer you up.'

'One wish?' said the farm wife.

'One,' he replied.

'Very well,' said the farm wife. 'Here's my wish. Since I don't believe in fairy godmothers, I wish you'd go back where you came from and leave me alone.'

This wish caught the Devil off guard and before he knew it he had landed with a bump in his throne room in Hell. Up he rose, his hair on end with anger. 'That's one I'll get someday, anyway,' he said to himself, and back he went to the World to find another victim.

The next soul he met was a very old man who sat under a tree staring away at nothing.

'Good morning, old man,' said the Devil in his best fairy-godmother voice. 'It's a fine day, isn't it?'

'One of many,' said the old man. 'One of many.'

The Devil didn't like this answer at all. It sounded too contented. 'See here then,' he said to the old man. 'I will grant you one wish—anything at all—but I can guess what you'll choose to wish for.'

'What's that?' said the old man.

'Why,' said the Devil, 'seeing as your life is nearly done, my guess is you'll wish to be a boy again.'

The old man pulled at his whiskers for a while and then he said, 'No, not that. It was good to be a boy, but not *all* good.'

'Then,' pursued the Devil, 'you'll wish to return to young manhood.'

'No,' said the old man. 'It was good to be a young man, but still—it was difficult, too. No, that wouldn't be my wish.'

The Devil began to feel annoyed. 'Well then,' he said, 'surely you'll wish to be once more in your prime, a hearty soul of forty or fifty.'

'No,' said the old man, 'I wouldn't wish that. It was good to be forty and good to be fifty, but those times were often hard as well.'

'What age will you wish to be, then?' barked the Devil, losing his patience at last.

'Why should I want to be any age but this one?' said the old man. 'That was *your* idea. One time is as good as another, and just as bad, too, for that matter. I'd wish for something different—I don't know what—if I really had a wish.'

'Well,' said the Devil, 'I've changed my mind anyway. You *don't* have a wish.'

'I didn't think I did,' said the old man, and he went back to staring away at nothing.

The Devil ground his teeth and smoke came out of his ears, but he went on down the road until at last he came to a vain young man in fancy clothes riding on a big brown horse. 'Good morning, young man,' said the Devil in his best fairy-godmother voice. 'It's a fine day, isn't it?'

'Indeed it is, dear madam,' said the vain young man, taking off his hat and bowing as well as he could from the saddle.

'Well now,' said the Devil, 'you're such a fine young man, I think I'll grant you a wish. One wish, anything you like. What do you say to that?'

'A wish?' cried the vain young man, dropping his hat. 'Anything I want? Can it really be true?'

'It can,' said the Devil, smiling. 'What will you wish for?'

'Dear me!' said the vain young man. 'Anything at all? I could wish to be rich, couldn't I!'

'You could,' said the Devil.

'But on the other hand I could wish that all the girls would fall in love with me,' said the vain young man, beginning to grow excited. 'Or I could wish to be the Crown Prince. Or the King! I could even wish to rule the whole World, as far as that goes.'

'You could,' said the Devil, smiling more than ever.

'Or I could wish to stay young and handsome forever,' said the vain young man.

'You could,' said the Devil.

'But wait!' cried the vain young man. 'Perhaps it would be better to wish for perfect health. What good are all those other things if you're too sick to enjoy them?'

'True,' said the Devil.

'Oh dear,' moaned the vain young man, wringing his hands. 'What to wish for! What to choose! I shall go quite mad, trying to decide! Health, power, money, love, endless youth, each a perfect wish all by itself. Sweet fairy godmother, I wish you'd *tell* me what to wish for!'

'If that's what you want, all right,' said the Devil with a smile as big as the moon. 'Most people think the best wish of all is to wish that every wish they ever wish will always come true.'

The young man's eyes grew round and his cheeks paled. 'Yes. Yes!' he said. 'They're right, of course. That *is* the best. All right, so here I go. I wish that every wish I ever wish will always come true.'

'Too late,' said the Devil gleefully.

The young man stared. 'Too late?' he cried. 'But why? You said I could wish for anything, didn't you?'

'I did,' grinned the Devil. 'That's true. But you used up your wish when you wished I'd tell you what to wish for!'

And with the young man's wail of anguish ringing in his ears, the Devil went back down to Hell, well satisfied at last.

A Tale of Two Frogs

ANNE SUTER

Once upon a time there was a king who had two daughters. Or, to be strictly accurate, he had a daughter and a stepdaughter, and if you know anything about stories which begin 'Once upon a time', you will already be taking sizeable bets that his real daughter was pretty, sweet, and gentle, and that his stepdaughter was a nasty bit of work, and ugly with it—and you'll be on an odds on winner.

King Phospherous' real daughter, Princess Primula, besides being pretty, was also obedient, dutiful and kind. She even tried to be kind to her stepsister, Princess Gorgonzola, which was pretty uphill work, because Gorgonzola not only had a face that would close down a factory at twenty paces, but she had a character to match, and at the drop of a coronet would go moaning off to her mother

to complain about Primula. Queen Grizelda was not exactly a *wicked* stepmother, but she was the next worst thing: disagreeable, greedy, and with a nature so acid you could have used it to cure wasp stings.

So whenever Gorgonzola came whinging to her that Primula had had a fuller glass of nectar or a larger slice of ambrosia, she would rush off and thump on King Phospherous' study door and demand retribution. The King, whose only interest in life was his stamp collection, would murmur, 'Yerse, yerse, m'dear—I'll see to it,' and Grizelda would continue to thump and scream until he would reluctantly tear himself away from his Illyrian Penny Blacks and tidy up his Never Never Land purple Triangulars and shuffle off in search of Princess Primula. Together they'd have a cosy little chat about the

weather and what might win the King Cophetua Stakes if the going was good, then Phospherous would potter back to his study and Primula would rub her eyes very hard to look as though she'd been crying, and creep back to her room under the beady gaze of Gorgonzola and Grizelda.

As these outbursts became more and more frequent, Primula became more and more fed up. Her eyes were getting positively bloodshot from so much rubbing, and as she never seemed to be able to please her stepmother and sister she decided the only way to escape them was to get married. This was easier said than done, because although

eligible princes were often invited to the palace, however longingly their eyes might stray to Primula it was always made perfectly plain to them that Gorgonzola, being the elder, had to be got off the shelf first.

Then Primula had A Great Idea.

Now, in all honesty, it must be said that though Primula was sweet, kind, and gentle, she was also not very bright. It would be an unkind exaggeration to say that she was thick as two short planks, but if you said *one* short plank you wouldn't be far off the mark. So it wasn't really surprising that her Great Idea was to find a handsome Prince who had been turned into a

frog, turn him back again and elope with him. (Come to think of it, perhaps two short planks isn't an exaggeration.) With this end in view she took to spending all her free time by the pond at the bottom of the palace garden, trying to chat up the frogspawn. Not unnaturally she didn't have a great deal of success, and there was no marked improvement in the conversational give and take when the frogspawn became tadpoles, and even Princess Primula was beginning to lose faith in her Great Idea. Then one day, when she arrived rather dejectedly at the pond—lo! all the tadpoles had turned into frogs and were hopping

about all over the place. Princess Primula, selecting one she thought particularly handsome, sat down and began to ply him with questions.

'What is your name?' she asked. 'And who gave you that name, and what Kingdom do you come from?' Reasonably enough she got no reply but, nothing daunted, she chattered on until another frog, who was sitting on a nearby stone and watching her sardonically, broke into her monologue.

'It's no good talking to *him*,' said this second frog, 'he can't speak English.' Now you or I might have been a shade disconcerted by this phenomenon, but to dear, dim-witted

Princess Primula it all seemed perfectly natural. It was just her Great Idea coming to fulfilment.

'Oh,' she squealed, 'how wonderful! *You* really can speak.'

'So can I,' said a third frog, not to be outdone. And Princess Primula was so overwhelmed with joy that she scooped the third frog up in the palm of her hand and kissed the top of his head, whereupon the frog broke into a great big grin.

'I say,' he explained, 'you've broken the spell!'

'You mean,' said Primula eagerly, 'that you're really a handsome prince who has been turned into a frog by a sorcerer's magic?'

'That's the ticket,' said the third frog. 'There's a wizard over at Nether Wackington with a frightfully limited range, so whenever he runs out of ideas he just goes back to turning handsome princes into frogs. There's dozens of us, all hanging about waiting to be kissed by princesses so that we can turn back again. Not,' he added, with a marked lack of humility, 'that they're all *quite* as handsome as I am. You've really had quite a bit of luck, singling me out.'

The second frog snorted at this and said, 'Humph, it's all a matter of taste, mate. You're not exactly Robert Redford you know, and there's a chap three ponds away who, in my opinion,

makes you look like Ken Dodd. Please don't think,' he added quickly, turning to Primula, 'that I'm gay or anything. It's just that I've got an artistic eye.'

'Of *course* not,' beamed Primula, who was so dim that she didn't even know what he was talking about. 'Oh, and I *do* apologize to you. It seems a bit unfair that I actually kissed *him*, because I saw *you* first. I'm afraid it was just the excitement.' If the second frog had had shoulders he would have shrugged them.

'Think nothing of it,' he said, 'no hard feelings. It's like I always say, you win some, you lose some. The name's Ferdinand, by the way,' he added, 'and if I can be of any assistance to you two, just drop me the word.'

'How *kind* you are,' gushed Primula. 'I'm sure we can get along splendidly now, but why,' she went on a bit anxiously, 'now that I've kissed him, doesn't he go on and turn back into a handsome prince?'

'Ah, yes, well, there's a bit more to it than that,' said the third frog. 'And by the way, *my* name is Prince Charming. A bit hackneyed I'm afraid, but eldest son and all that, had to be named after the Pater, you know. Unfortunately the family is a bit trad.—but rich,' he went on quickly, in case Primula was cooling off. 'Anyway, I was going to explain. When you kissed me you broke the spell, but I won't actually turn back

into a handsome prince—well, moderately handsome,' he corrected himself, catching Ferdinand's eye upon him, 'until you've married me and kissed me on our wedding night. After that you can kiss that dragonfly over there, and it will turn back into my horse, and then we'll ride off to my kingdom and live happily ever after. It all sounds a bit complicated, I'm afraid, but it actually does work, because the same thing happened to one of my cousins, and he's been happily married for ages now, with three offsprings. All children,' he added hastily, 'not frogs. Is that all right with you?' he enquired anxiously. 'I'm afraid it means taking rather a lot on trust.'

'Of *course* it is,' burbled Primula, who was the sort of girl who would not only have bought the Brooklyn Bridge, but would have told the man to keep the change. 'But I'll have to fly now,' she sighed, 'because I can hear the dinner gong ringing, and if I'm late they'll come to look for me. I'll be back just as soon as I can,' and so saying she danced off into the palace. The first person she met there was Gorgonzola, and because she was brimming over with joy, and because she really was remarkably stupid, she babbled out the whole story to her. Gorgonzola's eyes went snap, crackle and pop, and she seized Primula by the wrist.

'When does the wedding take place?' she hissed. Thick as she was, Primula realized she had been somewhat indiscreet, and tried to flannel a bit.

'Oh, we haven't named the day yet,' she said airily, 'and you won't tell anybody, will you?' she finished up anxiously.

'I won't tell a soul,' snapped Gorgonzola, and she meant it. She had every intention of going down to the pond at first light and nobbling Prince Charming for herself. He was, after all, already under starter's orders, Primula having broken the spell. All *she* had to do was whisk him past the winning post. What she hadn't realized was that Primula would go straight back to the pond after dinner. Charming was on the look out for her, and she sat down beside him and rattled on about Gorgonzola.

'You won't breathe a word to her about us, will you?' said Charming.

'But I've already told her,' said Primula. Because he had fallen deeply in love with her, Prince Charming didn't actually say, 'You blithering idiot,' but the end of his tongue got quite sore with being bitten.

'In that case,' he said, 'we'd better not hang about. We can't wait for a human parson, we'll have to make do with the local toad. It's all perfectly legal, he's a Justice of the Peace and he marries all the frogs around here. Is that all right?'

'But of course,' beamed Primula, who would quite happily have been married by a mushroom if she'd been told to. So the toad was hastily dragged from the bottom of the pond, with Ferdinand and the dragonfly as witnesses, then Primula kissed her frog bridegroom and he instantly turned into a handsome prince—well, anyway, fairly handsome. Then she kissed the dragonfly, who turned into a beautiful white charger, and they rode off at speed towards the castle wall. Unfortunately, as the dragonfly had for so long been used to having wings, he quite forgot to jump, which caused rather a disaster at the first attempt, but after a couple more refusals they eventually soared up over the castle wall and rode off into the sunset to live happily ever after. Whereupon Ferdinand yawned, shut his eyes and fell asleep on his stone.

He was awoken at dawn by a sharp prod of someone's foot in his ribs. He opened his eyes and saw Gorgonzola bending over him. He shuddered and quickly closed his eyes again. It was not a pretty sight.

'Wake up,' screeched Gorgonzola, 'I want some help. I'm looking for a frog that talks.'

'Well, I talk,' said Ferdinand, and almost before the words had left his mouth Gorgonzola had scooped him

up with a scream of joy, kissed him on the top of his head and said, 'Will you marry me?'

Ferdinand looked her up and down, shuddered again and said, 'What's in it for me?'

'Well,' said Gorgonzola, 'the palace is awfully comfortable, and we dine off gold plates every night, and as I'm the oldest daughter I can probably wangle it so that you'll be King one day.'

'OK, it's a deal,' said Ferdinand and, gloomily eyeing her up and down, added, 'got to take the rough with the smooth, I suppose. When do we ankle up the aisle?'

'Just as soon as Mummy can arrange it,' said Gorgonzola, and she bustled off

135

to burst into the Queen's boudoir.

'I'm engaged to be married,' she announced, and the Queen jumped for joy.

'Oh, my darling child,' she exclaimed, 'who's the lucky man?'

'Well, actually it's a frog,' said Gorgonzola.

After chucking a bucket of water over the Queen to revive her, Gorgonzola explained the situation, and by the end of her recital Grizelda's eyes were glinting greedily.

'But this is splendid news, my dear,' she said. 'You must be married immediately. In the circumstances though I think a *quiet* wedding would be best—so I don't think we'll bother dear Papa. He has just found an unperforated page of Lilliputian Lemon Yellows and I'm sure he wouldn't want to be disturbed. You run along and fetch your fiancé and I'll line up the Court Chaplain.'

The Court Chaplain was old and short-sighted, but not so old and short-sighted that he didn't know a frog when he saw one, and when Ferdinand came hopping up the aisle he staggered back a bit and hastily shuffled through the pages of the prayer book which tell you that you can't marry your cousin's aunt's stepfather. However, there didn't seem to be anything about frogs there, so he braced himself and got on with the service, only hesitating briefly over,

'Do you take this frog to be your wedded husband?'

Once he had pronounced them frog and wife, Gorgonzola grabbed Ferdinand, rushed hotfoot for her bedroom, plonked him on the pillow and kissed him. Ferdinand hopped back a couple of paces and wiped his front flipper across his mouth.

'I say,' he protested, 'I wish you wouldn't keep doing that. It's a terrible shock to the system.' But the Princess Gorgonzola wasn't really listening. She was just gazing at him expectantly, and Ferdinand gazed back unblinkingly.

'Well, go on then,' said Gorgonzola impatiently. 'Why don't you get on with it?'

'Get on with what?' asked the frog.

'When are you going to turn into a handsome prince?'

'A prince!' echoed Ferdinand. 'Have you gone bananas? I'm a frog, not a quick change artist!'

'But you're really a handsome prince who has been turned into a frog by a wicked wizard,' said Gorgonzola, with a touch of anxiety.

''*Course* I'm not,' said Ferdinand shortly. 'I'm just a FROG. Surely even you can see that.'

'But you can *talk*,' said Gorgonzola with gathering alarm.

'Well, that's not so difficult. A mate of mine taught me down in the pond.

Now he *was* a prince. Only last night a gorgeous bit of crumpet came and broke the spell and married him. Some people have all the luck,' he added with a depressed air. Inside the mind of Gorgonzola an awful, awful suspicion was beginning to take shape.

'Do you mean,' she screeched, 'do you actually mean,' she continued on a rising crescendo, 'can you *possibly* mean,' she screamed, 'that I'm actually married to a *FROG*?'

'Looks like it, old fruit,' croaked Ferdinand. 'It's like I always say, you win some, you lose some. You've made your bed, now you've got to lie on it—and speaking of which, all this excitement has made me a bit tired: I think I'll turn in now. Tell you what,' he added, gazing round appreciatively, 'these satin sheets are a bit of all right. Comfort-wise they beat pond slime all ends up,' and he flopped back on the pillows and fell asleep.

The Old Woman Who Lived in a Cola Can

BERNARD ASHLEY

Not all that long ago, and not so far away, there was an old woman who lived in a Cola can. 'All right,' you'd hear her say, 'the place *is* small, definitely chilly in December and scorching hot in July—but the floor never needs a coat of polish, and there's no dark corners where a spider can lurk.' The old woman reckoned it wasn't at all a bad place for a home, especially seeing there wasn't a penny to pay in rent.

One day, though, she went in for a telly, and she suddenly saw all sorts of things she'd never seen before. She saw all the adverts and loads of films—but instead of making her happy, all the new things only made her mad. She shouted and swore and shook her fist at the programmes.

'Rotten shame! Rotten shame! 'Tain't fair—it ain't fair!' she created. 'Why should I make do in this tinny little place when there's some lucky devils got nice flats in brand new tower blocks, with lifts to take them up and chutes to send the rubbish down? What's wrong with *me* I'd like to know? Why can't I have a chance to be choosy?'

She went on like that for ages, banging and clanging inside her can— till one day, by a stroke of luck just before her voice gave out, someone special heard her from the road: a flash young man who had won the pools and was looking for ways to get rid of his money.

He couldn't get across the grass to her quickly enough.

'Gordon Bennett, darlin', what a noise, what a *girls and boys*! But I heard what you was shoutin', and I've got to say I do feel sorry. I do. I feel

choked, *prodded an' poked*. But say
no more, girl, an' just keep your
pecker up. Give us a couple o' days
for some wheelin' an' dealin',
watch out for the motor—an'
we'll see what we're gonna see!'

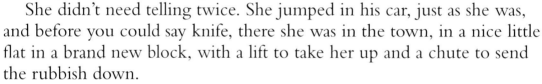

So the old woman said no
more. She switched off her telly,
kept her eyes glued to the road,
and before the milkman had
been round three times, the
flash young man was back,
sitting on his motor and calling
out across the grass.

'Come on, love, get out of
the can! Jump in the car, the
old *jam jar*, and come along o' me. I'll soon sort you out.'

She didn't need telling twice. She jumped in his car, just as she was,
and before you could say knife, there she was in the town, in a nice little
flat in a brand new block, with a lift to take her up and a chute to send
the rubbish down.

And she was over the moon with delight. But she clean forgot to say
thank you to the flash young man. And anyway, he had shot off to get on
with his spending. He'd gone to the races, and smart sunny places, to
Catterick, Corfu, and Crete. But after a while, when his mouth ached with
smiling, he thought he'd go back to see how the old woman was getting on.

And what did he hear when he got there? The tinkle of friendly tea-
cups, a few contented sighs like the summer wind in net curtains?

Not a bit of it. Just the slamming of doors and shouts enough to wake
the caretaker.

'Rotten shame! Rotten shame! 'Tain't fair—it ain't fair! I'm just about
up to *here*, miles off the ground in this poky little flat—when there's some
folks in the know got houses in streets, and their own front gates, with
cars out the front and patios round the back. What's wrong with *me*, I'd
like to know? Why don't I get the chance to be superior?'

The flash young man listened to every word she said. He kept dead quiet till he'd heard everything: then he put his eye to the spy-hole and he shouted through the door.

'Cheer up, doll,' he pleaded, 'no need for all that. Say no more, girl, and keep your pecker up. Give us a couple o' days for some wheelin' an' dealin', watch out for the motor—an' we'll see what we're gonna see!'

So the old woman said no more. She stopped banging doors, kept her eyes on the parking-bays, and before the kids had ruined the lifts three more times, the young man was back, leaning on his bonnet and calling up at her balcony.

'Come on, love, get down them stairs! Jump in the motor, the old *haddock an' bloater*, and come along o' me. I'll soon sort you out.'

She didn't need telling twice. She ran down the stairs, jumped in the back, and before she could say Jack Robinson, there she was in a neat town house in a proper little street, with car out front and a patio round the back.

She was over the moon with delight. But she clean forgot to say thank you to the flash young man. And, anyway, he'd shot off to get on with his

spending. He'd gone to casinos and sporting club beanos, to Monte, Majorca, and Maine. But after a while, when his hand hurt with winning, he thought he'd go back to see how the old woman was getting on.

And what did he hear when he got there? The contented creak of an old cane chair, the sound of soft singing to Radio Two?

Not a bit of it. Just the slam of a swing-bin being attacked and shouts which ran to the end of the road.

'Rotten shame! Rotten shame! 'Tain't fair—it ain't fair! Here am I shunted off in this common little house—when there's some people live it up in tree-lined cul-de-sacs, with nicely spoken neighbours and a man to do the grass. What's wrong with *me*, I'd like to know? When do I get a chance to be posh?'

The flash young man heard everything she said, then he rang upon her chimes.

'Heaven help us, love, what a state! What a terrible *two-an'-eight*! We can't have this. Give us a couple of days for some wheelin' an' dealin', watch out for the motor— an' we'll see what we're gonna see!'

So the old woman said no more. She stopped kicking-in the kitchen and packed her bags instead. And before she'd carried the dustbin through three times the flash young man was back, elbow on the dashboard and tooting at the door.

'Come on, love, leg it over that gate! Jump in the Bentley, the old *gently-gently*, and come along o' me. I'll soon sort you out.'

She didn't need telling twice. She slammed herself into the car with her hat in her hand, and before she could say one o'clock, there she was in a double-fronted house in a cul-de-sac, with nicely spoken neighbours and a man to do her grass.

And she was over the moon with delight. But she clean forgot to say thank you to the flash young man. And anyway, he'd shot off to get on with his spending. He bought up some pubs and three football clubs, United, Juventos and York. But after a while, when he got fed up with watching other people run around, he thought he'd go back and see how the old woman was getting on.

And what did he hear when he got there? The plop of fresh coffee being poured for the vicar, the rinsing of hands to get spoon polish off?

Not a bit of it. Just the rip of a radiator off of a wall and shouts loud enough to divert the traffic.

'Rotten shame! Rotten shame! 'Tain't fair—it ain't fair. Here am I overlooked in this middle-class place, when Lords and Ladies have mansions in big country parks, and servants to send off to Harrods. What's wrong with *me*, I'd like to know? When do I get the chance to be Upper Crust?'

The flash young man caught every word she said, then made his way round the back.

'Hold your horses! Half-time!' he called through the tradesmen's entrance. 'You'll make yourself sick, *Uncle Dick*! Say no more, girl, and keep your pecker up. Give us a couple of days for some wheelin' an' dealin', watch out for the motor—an' we'll see what we're gonna see!'

So the old woman said no more. She put a few favourite bits into a suitcase—and by the time she'd turned three collecting-tins away from her door, the flash young man was back, purring into the driveway and breaking the beam on her burglar alarm.

'Come on, love, let's move it. Jump in the Jag, the old *boast an' brag*, and come along o' me. I'll soon sort you out.'

She didn't need telling twice. She shot in as fast as the speed of greased lightning, and before she could say hell for leather there she was in a mansion, a duchess no less, with servants to send off to Harrods and a tiara to put on her head.

And she was over the moon with delight. But she clean forgot to say thank you to the flash young man. And, anyway, he'd shot off to get on with his spending. He bought up an airway to make a cheap fare-way for tourists on trips to the States. But after a while, when he got fed up with being pointed at, he thought he'd go back and see how the old woman was getting on.

And what did he hear when he got there? The click of a croquet ball sent through a hoop, the flow of a pool being filled?

Not a bit of it. Just the sound of a summer-house being destroyed, and shouts loud enough for three counties to hear.

'Rotten shame! Rotten shame! 'Tain't fair—it ain't fair. Here am I just a two-bob old duchess down here, when there's SOMEONE WE KNOW with a crown on her head! What's wrong with *me*, I'd like to know? When do I get the chance to be Royal?'

The flash young man took note of what the old woman said, then he made an appointment to see her.

'Your Grace, what a row! What a *bull and a cow*! You are comin' on strong. But I know what you mean, so you don't need to say another word. Give us a couple o' days for some wheelin' and dealin', watch out for the motor—and we'll see what we're gonna see!'

So the old woman said no more. She threw her tiara into the pool, kept her eyes peeled for the car with no number, and before she had time to sack three of her maids, the flash young man was back, gliding up towards her in his blue Rolls-Royce.

'Come on, ma'am,' he invited. 'Jump into the Roller, the *top hat an' bowler*, and come along o' me. I'll soon sort you out.'

She didn't need telling twice. She got into the back, cocked her head on one side, and started waving away out of this window and that. And before she could say, 'It gives me great pleasure,' she was there.

Back in her home in the Cola can: where, yell as she liked, she lived for the rest of her life.

But she never saved up for a telly again—and she wouldn't have said thank you if you'd given her one.

Paw Won't Like This

VANCE RANDOLPH

One time, there was a farm boy coming to town with a big load of hay. Just after they crossed the Cow Creek bridge, the horses got to acting up, and pretty soon they upset the whole business in the road just below the Applegate place. When old man Applegate come out, there was the wagon laying on one side, and a pile of hay big as a mountain. The farm boy was running around wild-eyed, and looked like he was going to bust out crying.

'Paw won't like this,' says he. 'Paw won't like this at all!'

As soon as he seen the horses wasn't hurt, old man Applegate done his best to get the boy calmed down. 'Don't you worry, son,' says he. 'It ain't your fault. Things like that might happen to anybody.' So then he says, 'You just fetch the team up to my barn, and come and eat dinner with us. After dinner me and the hired man will help you pitch that hay back on to the rack.'

The boy says he'd like to have dinner, but his paw wouldn't want him to leave the wagon.

'Don't you worry about that,' says old man Applegate. 'I've knowed your paw longer than you have, and I'll tell him all about it.' So the boy took his team up to the barn, and fed them. And then he went over to the house and ate a big dinner with the family.

After dinner they all set out on the porch awhile, a-belching and picking their teeth. Everybody tried their best to cheer the boy up, but he acted

terrible uneasy. 'Paw won't like this,' says he, 'I better go back to the wagon.'

The folks just laughed, and says for him not to worry.

'The first time I see your paw, I'll tell him you ain't to blame,' says old man Applegate. 'Maybe I'll tend to it this evening. Is your paw in town today?'

The boy looked at old man Applegate kind of bewildered. 'Why no,' he says, 'paw's under that there hay.'

Three Deaf Men

TRADITIONAL

Once a deaf man lost some goats. While he was looking for them he came upon another man mending a fence.

'Have you seen any goats wandering about?' he asked.

But the second man was deaf too.

'Most of the week I should think,' he said. 'It needs doing as far as the wood over there.' He pointed to the wood.

'Thank you very much,' said the first man as he set off towards it.

It so happened that he found his goats in the wood, so he rounded them up and herded them back along the road.

'I'm very grateful to you,' he said to the man mending the fence. 'If I hadn't found them when I did they would have wandered off and I'd have lost them for good.'

'Yes, at least that far,' said the fencer. 'I see you've got some goats,' he added, nodding towards them.

'You can have the one with the crumpled horn,' said the goat man, 'for all the help you've given me. She looks a little odd, I know, but she's all right in spite of that.' He pushed the goat towards the other man.

'I never touched it,' the man said. 'I'm sorry if it's been hurt, but it's nothing to do with me.'

'Three!' exclaimed the goat man. 'That's ridiculous! I'm glad to have them back, but I can't possibly let you have three goats. You can have that one with pleasure though.' And he pointed to it again.

'I tell you I didn't! I've never seen it before.'

'No, I'm not going to give you any more.'

'I can see it is, but I tell you it wasn't me!'

As they began to get more and more annoyed with each other, a third man came along the road riding a bicycle. They stopped him.

'This fellow's blaming me because one of his goats has been hurt,' said the fencer.

'He wants me to give him three of my goats just because he told me where to find them!' said the other.

'Yes I did,' said the cyclist. 'It was in the ditch back there and I didn't think it belonged to anyone.'

He got off the bike and handed it over to the other two.

'You should take care of your things,' he said as he walked off down the road. 'You'll be losing your goats next.'

Miss Jones

JAMES MARSHALL

Miss Jones had just settled down to a mug of milky tea and a plate of biscuits, when the telephone rang.

'I might have known,' she complained. 'Someone always calls when I'm having treats.'

Miss Jones waddled over to the telephone and picked up the receiver.

'Hello,' she said, somewhat irritably.

'Well?' said her friend Rose, who lived in the building. 'What are they like, your new neighbours across the hall in 12E? The postman said a couple moved in during the night.'

'I haven't heard a thing,' said Miss Jones, 'but my hearing isn't what it used to be.'

'I'm dying to know what they look like,' said Rose. 'Why don't you peek out into the hall and see what you can see?'

'You know how dark the hall is,' said Miss Jones, 'and besides, my eyesight isn't so good. I can't see my beak in front of my face.'

'Well, as soon as you hear anything at all, give me a call,' said Rose. And she hung up.

Miss Jones nibbled on her biscuits and sipped her milky tea.

'New neighbours,' she said. 'I do hope we get along.'

When she had finished her snack, she took the dishes into the kitchen to wash up.

'Moving is such hard work,' she said, 'I think I'll heat up some

vegetable soup and take it over. That will be a friendly gesture.'

When the soup was ready, Miss Jones stepped across the hall. It took her some time to locate the bell.

'Who is it?' called out a deep female voice.

'It is Miss Jones from across the hall,' said Miss Jones. 'I've brought you some vegetable soup.'

The door of 12E opened, but just a crack.

Miss Jones could not see the long furry nose protruding out, or the long, sharp white teeth.

'I thought you might be too tired to cook,' said Miss Jones.

'We *can't* cook yet,' said the new neighbour. 'The gas company hasn't turned on the gas. Otherwise . . .'

'Well then,' said Miss Jones, holding out the pot of soup, 'I hope you'll enjoy this.'

'Thanks,' said the new neighbour.

Miss Jones squinted and stepped closer to the open door.

'I really can't see you very well,' she said, 'this hallway is so dark.'

'My husband and I are canaries,' said the new neighbour quickly.

'Oh, how lovely,' said Miss Jones. 'But you don't sound like canaries.'

'We have low voices,' said the neighbour.

'But we *are* canaries,' said a deep male voice from behind the door. 'We are the Carusos.'

'I'm so pleased to meet you,' said Miss Jones. 'When you are all settled in, we must get together for dinner.'

The Carusos both gasped.

'By all means!' said Mrs Caruso. 'We'd like nothing better.'

'I'll be off now,' said Miss Jones. 'Toodleloo.'

'Toodleloo,' said the Carusos.

Miss Jones went inside her apartment. Charming couple, she thought.

Mrs Caruso closed the door to 12E. 'If only that stove had been working!' she said.

That evening Miss Jones consulted her calendar.

'My stars,' she said. 'Christmas is only two days away. I really must start planning my big Christmas dinner.'

But then she remembered that this Christmas her friend Rose would be out of town visiting her family.

'It will be a lonely Christmas indeed,' said Miss Jones. 'But I'll make the best of it.'

The doorbell rang.

'Who is it?' called out Miss Jones, who never opened the door without knowing who was on the other side.

'It is I, Mrs Caruso,' said the new neighbour.

Miss Jones threw open the door. 'Do come in,' she said.

'I only have a minute,' said Mrs Caruso, remaining in the dark hall. 'My husband and I were hoping you'd join us for Christmas dinner. It would give us such pleasure.'

Miss Jones was thrilled.

'I should be delighted!' she exclaimed. 'May I bring anything?'

'Just yourself,' said Mrs Caruso, and she hurried back into her own apartment.

'What a lovely surprise,' said Miss Jones, closing and bolting her door.

The next morning the telephone rang.

'Well?' said Rose. 'Have you met them yet?'

'Oh yes,' said Miss Jones. 'They are delightful. Canaries, you know. And they have invited me for Christmas dinner.'

'Marvellous,' said Rose. 'Now I don't have to worry about you being all alone.'

No sooner had Miss Jones hung up the telephone than it rang again.

It was Mrs Caruso. 'I hate to bother you, my dear,' she said, 'but do you by any chance have a nice big roasting pan? Ours seems to have been lost in the move.'

'Why certainly,' said Miss Jones. 'Is there anything else you need?'

'As a matter of fact,' said Mrs Caruso, 'would you know a good recipe for plum sauce?'

'I surely do,' replied Miss Jones. 'And why don't you allow me to make it? I'd so love to contribute to the dinner.'

'If you like,' said Mrs Caruso.

There was a short pause.

'I *do* hope I don't ruin the wild rice again this year,' said Mrs Caruso.

Miss Jones insisted on preparing the wild rice as well. 'I'd be happy to do it,' she said. 'You just concentrate on the main course.'

'Oh we will,' said Mrs Caruso.

Miss Jones felt it would be impolite to ask what the main course would be. 'I'm sure it will be tasty.'

On Christmas Eve Mrs Caruso called again with a slight problem.

'The gas company still hasn't turned on the stove,' she said. 'I don't know *what* we're going to do!'

Miss Jones had the solution immediately.

'But you must use mine,' she said.

'You are kind. What would we do without you?' said Mrs Caruso. 'Have the oven good and hot about noon.'

'We can have eggnog while we're waiting for dinner,' said Miss Jones.

Mrs Caruso thought this was an excellent idea, although she confessed that eggnog was really not one of her specialities.

On Christmas morning the Carusos were up bright and early.

'This is going to be a Christmas to remember!' said Mr Caruso.

'Yum, yum, yum!' said his wife. 'I hope there will be plenty of plum sauce.'

In her own apartment, Miss Jones, who had got up even earlier, was merrily setting the table.

'I have such pretty china,' she said.

At noon on the nose, the Carusos rang the doorbell, and Miss Jones opened the door.

'Merry Christmas!' she said.

'Merry Christmas!' said the Carusos, stepping inside. 'Is the oven nice and hot?'

'Oh dear, oh dear,' said Miss Jones. 'I *knew* I'd forget something.'

The Carusos were quite put out, but they tried not to show it.

'No harm done,' said Mrs Caruso. 'Turn it on right now. We'll start on the eggnog.'

Miss Jones went into the kitchen and came back shortly.

'It won't take long to heat up,' she said.

'Good,' said the Carusos.

Conversation did not flow easily.

'Nice day,' said Mr Caruso.

'Very nice indeed,' said Miss Jones, 'and so lovely to share it with new neighbours.'

'Yes,' said the Carusos.

'I think I'll go see about the oven,' said Mrs Caruso, and she got up to go into the kitchen. Suddenly Miss Jones felt a long furry tail brush up against her feet as Mrs Caruso passed.

Oh no, thought Miss Jones, the Carusos aren't canaries at all!

And right away she saw what was up.

'Miss Jones, dear,' Mrs Caruso called out from the kitchen. 'Would you step in here a minute?'

Miss Jones knew she had to do some fast talking—or else!

'I'm sure you can take care of everything,' she answered back. 'You don't need me. Come have another cup of eggnog.'

Mrs Caruso returned.

'The oven is ready,' she said, giving her husband a significant look.

'I'm sure I won't be able to eat more than a few bites,' said Miss Jones. 'Ever since my operation I haven't had much appetite.'

'Operation?' said the Carusos.

'Actually, I've had several,' said Miss Jones. 'They took out my gizzard.'

'Not the gizzard!' said Mr Caruso, who'd always been partial to gizzards.

'And I have only a tiny bit of my liver left,' said Miss Jones. 'Hardly anything at all.'

'That's really too bad!' said the Carusos.

'Of course,' said Miss Jones, 'my doctor does want me to put on weight. I'm just a bag of bones.'

'You look pretty plump to me,' said Mrs Caruso.

'Feathers,' said Miss Jones. 'Merely feathers, very deceptive.'

The Carusos could now see their big Christmas dinner vanishing before their very eyes.

Miss Jones began to scratch frantically.

'Do excuse me,' she said. 'I know it's rude to do this in company, but I have such a flea problem.'

'You don't say,' said the Carusos.

Miss Jones continued.

'Of course,' she said, 'I'm not implying I don't have absolute faith in my doctor, but I do wish he wouldn't give me all that medicine. I'm positively *stuffed* with milk of magnesia.'

Now this was simply too much for the Carusos, and they hastily made their excuses.

'We hate to run off like this,' said Mr Caruso, 'but we forgot we always visit house-bound people at Christmas.'

Miss Jones did not insist on their staying.

'We'll get together in the new year,' she said.

'Of course,' said the Carusos (if that was their real name), and they hurried off, hoping to find *something* decent to eat for Christmas.

'You and your bright ideas!' mumbled Mr Caruso.

Miss Jones bolted the door, collapsed on the sofa, and heaved great sighs of relief. Then she placed a call to her landlord, who was shocked to learn he had wolves in the building.

'I shall remedy this situation immediately, Miss Jones,' he said.

Miss Jones felt reassured and vowed to open her door to no one until she was advised that the Carusos had departed for good.

That night she sat down to a big plate of plum sauce.

'I really shouldn't,' she said. 'My doctor says I'm a little overweight, but sometimes we need to reward ourselves.'

And she ate it all.

There Ain't Been No News

RICHARD AND JUDY DOCKREY YOUNG

Once there was a man down in Fort Smith, Arkansas, that ran a 'feed, seed, and everything you need' store, but in order to do his business he travelled a lot by train. When he'd go away he'd get his cousin Fred to look after the farm chores for him. Well, he was gone for weeks one time, and came home, and he'd wired Fred to meet him at the station.

'Fred,' he said when he saw him, 'what's the news?'

'Oh, Henry,' said Fred, 'there ain't been no news.'

'You mean to say there ain't been no news, and me gone for weeks?'

'Nope,' said Fred. 'There ain't been no news. Oh . . . except your dog died. But other than that, there ain't been no news.'

'My dog died?' said Henry. 'What happened to him?'

'Well, that's easy to explain,' said Fred. 'He ate too much burned horse meat. But other than that, there ain't been no news.'

'Wait a minute,' said Henry. 'Where'd my dog get ahold of burned horse meat?'

'Well, that's easy to explain,' said Fred. 'When your barn burned to the ground it killed all your livestock, and your dog got ahold of too much burned horse meat, and died. But other than that, there ain't been no news.'

'My barn burned?' said Henry. 'What caused my barn to burn?'

'Well,' said Fred, 'that's easy to explain. It was sparks. Sparks from the house set the barn ablaze, and killed all your livestock, and your dog got ahold of too much burned horse meat, and ate it, and died. But other than that, there ain't been no news.'

'Sparks from the house?' said Henry. 'What happened to my house? Did my house burn down?' Fred was nodding solemn-like. 'What burned my house down?'

'Oh, Henry, that's easy to explain,' said Fred. 'It was the candles, they set the curtains on fire. All them candles around the coffin. They set the curtains on fire and burned the house down, and sparks from the house set the barn ablaze, and the barn burned down and killed all your livestock, and your dog got ahold of too much burned horse meat, and died. But other than that, there ain't been no news.'

'*What coffin?*' hollered Henry, lifting Fred off the landing by his lapels. '*Who died?*'

'Now, Henry,' said Fred, 'that's easy to explain. Your mother-in-law died, and we had the wake in the parlour, and the candles set the curtains on fire and burned the house down, and the sparks from the house set the barn ablaze, and burned the barn down, and killed all your livestock, and your dog got ahold of too much burned horse meat, and ate it, and died. But other than that, there ain't been no news.'

'WHAT HAPPENED TO MY MOTHER-IN-LAW?' yelled Henry, shaking Fred around in the air.

'Oh . . . Henry . . . we've been arguing about that. Some says one thing and some says another. But as near as we can figure, she died of a broken heart when your wife ran off with the seed clerk.

'But other than that, there ain't been a bit of news!'

Acknowledgements

Marian Abbey: 'Digging for Trouble', © 1995 Marian Abbey. First published here by permission of the author.

Bernard Ashley: 'The Old Woman Who Lived in a Cola Can', first published in *Puffin Post*, 1984. Reprinted by permission of the author.

Natalie Babbitt: 'Wishes', from *The Devil's Storybook* by Natalie Babbitt. Copyright © 1974 by Natalie Babbitt. Reprinted by permission of Farrar, Straus & Giroux, Inc.

Richmal Crompton: 'The Outlaws and the Triplets', taken from *William the Pirate* by Richmal Crompton, first published 1932 © Richmal Ashbee, published by Macmillan Children's Books. Reprinted by permission of Macmillan Children's Books.

Mick Gowar: 'The Amazing Talking Pig', copyright © Mick Gowar, 1993. From *The Amazing Talking Pig and Other Stories*, first published by Hamish Hamilton Children's Books, 1993. Reproduced by permission of Penguin Books Ltd.

Dennis Hamley: 'Thank you, St Joseph's', © 1995 Dennis Hamley. First published here by permission of the author.

Irene Hedlund: 'Mighty Mountain and the Three Strong Women', © Irene Hedlund 1982, translated by Judith Elkin from *Stories Round the World* (Hodder & Stoughton, 1990). Reprinted by permission of A & C Black (Publishers) Ltd.

Florence Parry Heide: 'Ruby' from *Tales for the Perfect Child,* copyright © 1985 by Florence Parry Heide. Reprinted by permission of Piccadilly Press Ltd and Lothrap, Lee & Shepard Books, a division of William Morrow & Company, Inc.

Robin Klein: 'The Kidnapping of Clarissa Montgomery', from *Ratbags and Rascals,* first published in England by Oxford University Press, 1984. Reprinted by permission of Haytul Pty Ltd, c/o Curtis Brown (Aust) Pty Ltd, Sydney.

W. K. McNeil: 'Like Dog, Like Dad', from *Ozark Mountain Humor* edited by W. K. McNeil (August House, 1989). Copyright 1989 by W. K. McNeil. Reprinted by permission of August House Publishers Inc.

Jan Mark: 'The One That Got Away', from *Story Chest,* collection copyright © Barbara Ireson, 1986. Text copyright © Jan Mark. First published by Viking Kestrel Books, 1986. Reproduced by permission of Penguin Books Ltd.

James Marshall: 'Miss Jones', from *Rats on the Roof and Other Stories* by James Marshall. Copyright © 1991 by James Marshall. Reproduced by permission of Penguin Books Ltd, and Dial Books for Young Readers, a division of Penguin Books USA Inc.

Andrew Matthews: 'Excuses, Excuses', from *The Great Sandwich Racket and Other Stories,* copyright © Andrew Matthews, 1990. First

published by Blackie Children's Books, 1990. Reproduced by permission of Penguin Books Ltd.

Bel Mooney: 'I Don't Want to Wash', from *I Don't Want To* (Methuen, 1985). Reprinted by permisssion of David Higham Associates.

Michaela Morgan: 'Sick as a Parrot', © 1995 Michaela Morgan. First published here by permission of the author.

Lilith Norman: 'My Simple Little Brother and the Great Aversion Therapy Experiment'. Reprinted by permission of Lilith Norman, c/o Margaret Connolly & Associates Pty Ltd, Literary Agents.

Vance Randolph: 'Paw Won't Like This', from *The Talking Turtle and Other Ozark Folk Tales* by Vance Randolph. Copyright © 1957 by Columbia University Press. Reprinted by permission of the publisher.

Robert Scott: 'Kevin Jackson', © 1995 Robert Scott. First published here by permission of the author. The following traditional tales have been retold for this collection by Robert Scott: 'Counting Noses', 'Why Cows Don't Fly', 'Three Deaf Men', 'The Hodja and the Poisoned Baklava', all © 1995 Robert Scott.

Anne Suter: 'A Tale of Two Frogs', Copyright © Anne E. Suter, 1987. Reprinted by permission of Jennifer Kavanagh on behalf of the author.

Ian Whybrow: 'Sniff, Miss Morris and a Bit of Cuckoo Spit', from *The Sniff Stories* by Ian Whybrow (Bodley Head, 1987). Reprinted by permission of Random House UK Ltd.

David Henry Wilson: 'Wolves 11 Rabbits 0', from *Yucky Ducky* by David Henry Wilson (J. M. Dent, 1988). Reprinted by permission of The Orion Publishing Group Ltd.

Richard and Judy Dockrey Young: 'The Old Mule Won't Work' and 'There Ain't Been No News', from *Ozark Tall Tales* collected and edited by Richard and Judy Dockrey Young (August House, 1989). Copyright 1989 by Richard and Judy Dockrey Young. Reprinted by permission of August House Publishers Inc.

While every effort has been made to trace and contact copyright holders this has not always been possible. If notified, the publisher will be pleased to rectify any errors or omissions at the earliest opportunity.

Artist Acknowledgements

Anni Axworthy: pp 51, 52/3, 110, 111, 112, 113, 115, 157

Caroline Crossland: pp 4, 5, 10, 11, 90, 91

Mei-Yim Low: pp 12, 13, 75, 77, 81, 116/17

Caroline Magerl: pp 38, 39, 40, 41, 42, 43, 46/7, 50, 104, 105, 106, 107, 109, 144, 145

Vince Reid: Jacket, endpapers, pp 1, 2, 3,28, 30, 31, 33, 34, 35, 36/7, 68, 69, 70, 72, 73, 118, 121, 123, 124, 125, 126, 127, 128, 138, 139, 140, 141, 143, 146, 147, 158, 159, 160

Martin Remphry: pp 14, 16, 17, 18, 19, 25, 26/7, 54, 55, 58/9, 61, 64, 67, 84, 87

Jamie Smith: pp 20, 23, 24, 82, 92, 93, 94, 95, 97, 99, 100/1, 102/3, 129, 130/1, 133, 135, 137, 148, 149, 151, 153, 155